Nijinsky

Nijinsky
GOD OF THE DANCE

DEREK PARKER
Foreword by Dame Ninette de Valois

First published 1988

© DEREK PARKER 1988

All rights reserved. No part of this book may be reproduced or utilized in any form or by any means, electronic or mechanical, including photocopying, recording or by any information storage and retrieval system, without permission in writing from the Publisher.

British Library Cataloguing in Publication Data
Parker, Derek
Nijinsky: God of the Dance.
Nijinsky, Vaslav 2. Ballet dancers—— Soviet Union —— Biography
I. Title
792.8'2'0924   GV1785.N6

ISBN 1-85336-032-5

Equation is an imprint of the Thorsons Publishing Group, Wellingborough, Northamptonshire, NN8 2RQ, England

Printed and bound in Great Britain by
Butler & Tanner Ltd, Frome and London

1 3 5 7 9 10 8 6 4 2

CONTENTS

Acknowledgements	7
Illustrations	8
Foreword: Dame Ninette de Valois	9
Introduction	13
I The Years of Promise 1889–1908	17
II Wonder of Wonders 1908–1909	47
III The Continuing Legend 1909–1911	71
IV The Choreographer 1911–1913	119
V The Fallen God 1913–1950	149
Selected Bibliography	188
Index	190

To Zdislaw and Maria Zazula with love

ACKNOWLEDGEMENTS

I am grateful to the following publishers for permission to quote from the books named:

A. & C. Black in respect of four passages from Cyril Beaumont's *The Diaghilev Ballet in London* (1940).

The BBC for permitting me to quote from my two radio programmes about Nijinsky and Diaghilev.

Jonathan Cape in respect of extracts from the *Diary of Vaslav Nijinsky* (ed. Romola Nijinsky, 1963).

Dance Horizons and Dance Books Limited in respect of two extracts from *Diaghilev Observed by Critics in England and the United States, 1911–29*, by Nesta Macdonald (1975).

Eric Glass Ltd in respect of a passage from Romola Nijinsky's *Nijinsky* (1936).

Macmillan in respect of a passage from Sir Osbert Sitwell's *Great Morning*.

John Murray in respect of two passages from Lydia Sokolova's *Dancing for Diaghilev*, edited by Richard Buckle (1960).

Harold Matson Company Inc. in respect of Boris Kochno's *Diaghilev and the Ballets Russes* (1971).

Weidenfeld and Nicolson in respect of two extracts from Richard Buckle's *Nijinsky* (1971).

ILLUSTRATIONS

The illustrations appear by kind permission of the following:

Dance Collection, The New York Public Library at Lincoln Center, Astor, Lenox and Tilden Foundations: 15, 26, 31, 34, 43, 46, 53, 57, 58, 60 (bottom), 62, 70, 72, 83, 84, 85, 86, 87 (bottom), 97, 98, 99 (top), 101, 102, 103, 104, 106, 107, 108, 109, 118, 123 (bottom), 125, 127, 142 (top and bottom), 144, 146 (top), 160, 166, 168.
Courtesy VOGUE copyright © 1917 (renewed 1945) by the Condé Nast Publications Inc.: 113.
Nesta Macdonald (private collection): 41, 51, 68, 99 (bottom), 111, 153, 161, 167.
By kind permission of the Trustees of the Victoria and Albert Museum: 28, 49, 55, 56, 59, 60 (top), 67, 69, 114, 121, 122, 123 (top), 128, 129, 130, 136, 137 (top and bottom), 139, 146 (bottom), 147, 152, 173, 175, 181.
The Raymond Mander & Joe Mitchenson Theatre Collection: 16, 32, 52 (bottom), 73, 87, 79, 81, 95 (bottom).
Derek Parker (private collection): 19, 20, 78, 94, 96, 100, 120, 148, 150, 178.

Every effort has been made to trace the ownership of all illustrations. We apologize for any error or omission.

FOREWORD

I only saw Nijinsky dance once...
I was very young when I went to Covent Garden to see *Les Sylphides*. I had been used to seeing Mikhail Mordkin, Pavlova's partner, a more august type of Russian male dancer. Suddenly here was this very small boy, with hair down to his shoulders and wearing a strange costume; I am afraid I turned to my mother and said 'I don't like that man.'

If we saw him dance now, he would perhaps not make the impression he did in his day. When you look at the photographs of him, so small and with those extraordinarily muscular legs and rather overdeveloped figure, I think today he would have been regarded as a wonderful virtuoso dancer and kept for such roles as the Bluebird. I can't see him in the great *classical* roles – indeed Diaghilev didn't use him a great deal in them, but kept him in virtuoso and distinguished *demi-charactère* parts.

He must have been wonderful and also a fine actor. Petrushka, after all, is a very demanding role requiring a lot of execution and interpretation and was mounted on him. We all wonder, now, just how high he *did* leap; but his technique must have been remarkable – flying through the window so easily at the end of *Spectre de la Rose*; that must have made a most sensational exit.

What he really did as a dancer was to place the male dancer once again in the position that he held in the days of Vestris. I think that today we might perhaps welcome him primarily as a choreographer. He evidently had a real talent, a talent a long way ahead of his time. Was there perhaps something of a problem with some of his ballets musically? I danced in *L'Après-Midi d'un Faune*, which is a ballet of his we know very well (both Marie Rambert and his sister Bronia Nijinska revived it – and his sister knew the choreography very well). In fact, when I was with Diaghilev, Bronia danced the Faune – the part became very sinister, danced by a woman!

The ballet did not seem to me to be a real interpretation of Debussy's score, somehow I personally felt it was a clever imposition on the music. It wasn't that the choreography was unmusical, rather it simply seemed, in a curious way, not to be a true reading of the music. Of course this is purely a private opinion, though I know that it was one shared by some of the music critics.

We cannot, I think, really know what *Le Sacre du Printemps* was like; but I did see *Jeux* once (when Nijinska revived it) and greatly enjoyed it. It was again in advance of its day, another indication that her brother had foresight as well as a great talent. *L'Après-Midi d'un Faune* is, after all, a remarkable work – it is simply the curious fact that I found no rapport with the music. The ballet itself I loved – loved to look at it.

I saw Nijinsky twice more, once when Diaghilev brought him to a rehearsal in Paris. His sister burst into tears, she said 'I can't take it, I can't take it.' She was terribly upset. She was a wonderful woman and I had a great admiration for her. Later he came to Covent Garden one evening with his wife when they were living in England after the war, he sat in a box to watch a performance. In the repertory that night was my ballet *Checkmate*. I thought Nijinsky wasn't really with us. When the audience clapped, he clapped – but one couldn't talk to him. However, Romola Nijinska said to me afterwards, 'He liked very much *Checkmate*.' I watched him during that particular work. He was leaning forward in his seat, more and more and more . . . I am not at all sure he knew what he was looking at, perhaps he may have played chess at some time in his life and there was a slowly awakened interest through memory? He came on to the stage afterwards and of course the company were wildly excited, but he didn't say anything.

We must remember that we had never seen a male dancer with such a fantastic jump until he leapt into our midst, and his elevation was his greatest sensation as a dancer. But I do think he was perhaps an even greater choreographer. There seems to me to be no doubt that if he were alive today, it would be his choreographic ideas we would be chasing rather than his great leaps.

Dame Ninette de Valois

INTRODUCTION

It is now over fifteen years since the publication of Richard Buckle's splendid biography of Nijinsky, and nine years since the relationship between the dancer and the impresario Diaghilev was explored in his equally thorough biography of the latter. Little has been published in the intervening years (with the exception of a translation of the first Russian biography), but as we approach the centenary of Nijinsky's birth it is perhaps time to look again at the man and the legend.

During the 1960s I was able to talk to most of the surviving members of Diaghilev's Ballets Russes then living in England – including the dancers Tamara Karsavina, Dame Marie Rambert, Lydia Sokolova and Stanislas Idzikowsky, the critic Cyril Beaumont, and the designer Grace Lovat Frazer, all of whom had either worked with Nijinsky or had seen almost all his performances in England. I also talked briefly about Nijinsky to his wife Romola and his sister Bronia. Fascinated by the legend of this obviously marvellous dancer and extraordinary man, I made notes of my conversations. All these people are now, alas, dead. Sir Sacheverell Sitwell also talked to me about his memories of the Ballets Russes and Nijinsky.

I have made use of these memories in this book, and of some material which appeared in Vera Krasovskaya's *Nijinsky*, published in Leningrad in 1974 and in an English translation in 1979. Although this is a somewhat esoteric production – she was forced by the political climate to disapprove volubly of such figures as Diaghilev and Prince Lvov, and unable even to mention the fact of

Left *When the Ballets Russes was in London in 1911, Lady Ripon took Nijinsky to the studio of the most fashionable portrait artist of the time, John Singer Sargent, who made this charcoal sketch of him in his head-dress for* Le Pavillon d'Armide, *strikingly recording his strange, equivocal sexuality.*

Nijinsky's homosexuality (let alone the source of the ballet *Jeux*) – there were several new facts gleaned from Nijinsky's few remaining Russian contemporaries and from Russian archives.

I have tried to eschew technicalities – I believe that most interested readers will be familiar with the few basic ballet terms which have seemed unavoidable.

Zofia Bartoszewska and the Panstwowy Instytut Wydarniczy in Warsaw gave invaluable assistance, and the London Library and its Librarian and assistants were, as usual, extremely helpful. I am especially grateful for the support and advice of my wife, who knows a great deal more about the techniques of the ballet than I.

In his autobiography, Michel Fokine wrote: 'I deeply regret that imaginary biographies have been written about that marvellous dancer, Nijinsky. If one were written telling the truth about him as a dancer, this would be a sufficiently beautiful picture of an artist, unencumbered by fairy tales and exaggerations.' This has been one of my aims in this book.

CHAPTER I

The Years of Promise 1889-1908

One morning in 1905, a promising young solo dancer of the Imperial Russian Ballet, Tamara Karsavina, was walking through the boys' practice studio in the Imperial Ballet School in Theatre Street, St Petersburg, when she saw a class of boys at work. Years later, she said:

'I saw the pupils all in rows, and I noticed that when the others all came down after their jumps, there was one in the back row who stayed up in the air! So I asked the teacher, Mikhail Oboukhov, "Now who is that boy? We never heard of him." "Ah," he said, "that is Nijinsky – and you soon will hear about him."'

Indeed, the whole world was to hear about Vaslav Nijinsky; over ninety years after his birth his is still one of the best-known names in the history of the twentieth-century ballet – a field of art which before him was, in the West, dominated almost entirely by women. Dame Marie Rambert, constantly asked about his style and achievement, was to say of him: 'I am often asked, "Did he really leap so high?" And my only reply is, I don't know how far from the ground, but I know it was near the stars.' Nijinsky's legendary leaps have tended indeed to distract attention from his other accomplishments – particularly his fine characterization and mime in a wide variety of roles, and his work as a choreographer. He was much more than a man who could jump very high and give the impression of hanging for a moment stationary in mid-air.

At the time of his birth, in 1888, ballet in the West was at a very low ebb indeed. The great age of the Romantic ballet – of Taglioni and Grisi, Cerrito

Left *Vaslav Nijinsky (1890–1950).*

and Elssler, and of the fine male dancers Lucien Petipa, Saint-Leon and Perrot – was over. Since the 1850s in France male dancing in particular had virtually died, and a new generation of ballerinas had failed to find a way into the affection of the public; audiences for ballet began to fall off both in Paris and London. Relatively few balletomanes travelled to Russia; if they had done so, they would have found a violently contrasting state of affairs, for there in St Petersburg Marius Petipa was consolidating a great ballet tradition which would enable Russia to lead the way to the glories of a great new age of dance.

Born in Marseilles, Petipa had been *maitre de ballet* of the Imperial Company. By the time he retired in 1904 he had produced over fifty new ballets – including *The Sleeping Beauty* and *Swan Lake* (in 1890 and 1895 respectively). To his company came many distinguished dancers from Italy, among them Virginia Zucchi, Carlotta Brianza and Enrico Cecchetti, whose spectacular leaps and turns attracted much attention – and whose reputation did a great deal to focus attention on the male dancers he was to encourage and teach.

The backbone of the Imperial company which danced at the beautiful Maryinsky Theatre (now the Kirov State Theatre) was a *corps de ballet* and a team of soloists trained at the Imperial Theatre School, founded in 1738 by Jean Baptiste Lande, a Frenchman who went to Russia to become balletmaster of a school for poor children. The Empress Anne later allowed him to start an Academy in rooms in the Winter Palace itself; she chose twelve boys and twelve girls herself to be the first pupils. The School, which still continues its proud tradition, was to train Nijinsky and his greatest partner, Karsavina, as well as the initially more famous Anna Pavlova.

Nijinsky's parents were two Polish dancers,

Thomas Lavrentievitch Nijinsky and Eleanora Nicolaevna (née Bereda).

Eleanora was born in Warsaw on 28 December 1856.* Her father, a compulsive gambler, died when he was relatively young, and his distraught widow a few weeks later, leaving three daughters and two sons with practically no means of support. The teenage sons Adam and Henryck, still students, cared for their sisters by making a slender income from spare-time tutoring. Two of the girls, Stephanie and Leonora (known as Stepha and Liota) secretly enrolled themselves in the Wielki Theatre ballet school, and made a little money by appearing as extras. When their brothers discovered their secret, there was a tremendous row: they considered that to be a ballet girl was to be little better than a whore. But – perhaps for financial reasons – they eventually withdrew their objections, and young Stepha at thirteen became a member of the *corps de ballet*, earning eight roubles a month. When, in 1868, she was 'discovered' by a Polish ballet-master who had come to Russia to recruit dancers for a season in Kiev, she signed a contract as soloist on condition that Liota (then only eleven) should be taken into the company.

The sisters were the youngest members of the company, and speaking only Polish, must have felt very isolated within a troup of Russian dancers. Stepha was immediately popular – and somewhat to her surprise, so was Liota, whose very youth and diminutive size caught at the hearts of audiences. On her twelfth birthday she was made an official member of the *corps*.

Back in Russia, the sisters danced their way around the country for several years. In 1876, Liota met an artillery captain with whom she fell in love,

Eleanora Nijinska (1856–1932), Vaslav's mother; perhaps a wedding photograph. She was a good character dancer, but retired early, giving dancing lessons to help keep her and her three children after estrangement from her husband.

---

*All dates are based on the Gregorian (New Style) calendar.

and announced her retirement from the stage – only to send the engagement ring back when she discovered that her fiancé had taken part in the repression of the Polish insurrection of 1863/4. She re-joined the ballet, and continued her career – until she met Thomas ('Foma') Nijinsky.

He had been born in Warsaw on 7 March 1862, and from the age of eight he also had been a pupil of the Wielki Theatre school. At eighteen he was dancing solo roles, and was sent to Odessa to appear in the opera ballet there. He soon realized that the prospect of employment in Russia was considerably better than in Poland, and though he was a passionate nationalist, he readily accepted the offer of a contract as soloist with the Odessa theatre. He applied for leave of absence from the Wielki, but instead received a curt letter of dismissal. This did not distress him too much – partly because by this time he and Liota were in love.

The only thing that stood in the way of an immediate marriage was the fact that all young Poles were liable to conscription. Apart from separating him from Liota, the prospect was dangerous to a dancer, whose technique would not be improved by a year's absence from class, and by the very different discipline of military drill. He reported to the military hospital for medical examination. As he stood stark naked waiting his turn, an apparent miracle occurred: he was told that the army could not cope with all the young men eligible for service, and that lots had been drawn for exemptions. He had drawn what for him was a lucky number. He rushed from the room, pulled on his trousers and shirt, and, leaving his underwear in the waiting-room, rushed back to his home to send a message to Liota. They could be married.

Only the fact that she was older than Foma delayed the occasion, but eventually, he won her round, and they were married in May 1884, in the

Thomas Lavrentievitch Nijinsky (1862–1912), father of Vaslav, an excellent dancer with a spectacular technique and a fine sense of drama. This is possibly a wedding-day photograph: he married Nijinsky's mother in 1884.

Caucasian port of Baku. She was twenty-seven; he was twenty-two.

Foma's career was secure: he was *premier danseur* and ballet-master, and Liota was a soloist with the touring Setov Opera company, which made its way by coach from city to city, town to town, much as in England the Victorian theatre companies toured in their own railway carriages. Not, perhaps, the easiest career in which to start a family: but at Tiflis on 29 December 1886, Stanislav Fomitch Nijinsky (known as Stassik) was born; and two years later, at Kiev, on 12 March 1889, Vaslav Fomitch (Vatsa) followed him. Not quite two years later, on 8 January 1891, Liota danced in the first act of Glinka's opera *A Life for the Tsar* at the Opera House in Minsky, then retired to a nearby hospital and gave birth to Bronislava Fominitchna (Bronia). The company was extremely surprised for, astonishing though it seems, no one had realized that Liota was pregnant.

The Setov company settled into repertory in Kiev between September and the end of May, which at least allowed the Nijinskys a little settled home life before the adventures of the summer, when Foma and Liota set out to busk their way from theatre to theatre, or – as in the summers of 1892 and 1893 – to settle on the island of Trukhanov, not far from Kiev, where they worked in summer theatre. The family was comfortably off – they could, for instance, afford servants, including a nurse for the three children – and life was pleasant enough. For the eight-month season of 1893/4 they went to Odessa, where Foma and Liota appeared with the Opera Theatre, and in their spare time gave ballroom dancing lessons both to children and adults. The Nijinsky boys naturally joined the children's classes, and Foma soon began to teach them little solo dances. Both Stassik and Vatsa appeared in an amateur performance at Easter, Vatsa taking the girl's role in a *hopak*. It was his first public performance.

At the beginning of the year, Josef Yakovelevitch Setov died, and his company was disbanded at the end of the season. Foma had no difficulty in forming his own company, with some of the many dancers with whom he had appeared as its *corps*. He engaged the Italian ballerina Maria Giuri as his principal artiste, and, raising money by pawning many of the family's possessions, rented a theatre for a single performance. It was a success, but it was impossible to find bookings – partly at least because of the reported impending death of the Tsar, which inhibited attendance at all theatres. The company broke up, and the Nijinskys once more found themselves travelling Russia like gypsies, dancing wherever they could procure engagements – at St Petersburg, Novorossiysk, Ekaterinodar, Vladikavkaz and Nijni Novgorod (where they worked in *Café Chantant*).

The children had had a taste of dancing lessons, but at first it remained only a taste; Foma was simply too busy to teach his children – though they were taught some steps by two travelling black American music-hall tap-dancers, Johnson and Johnson. Bronia and Vatsa were fascinated by their showy satin coats and top hats – but even more by the rhythms of their dances.

Soon, however, Foma began to give Vatsa and Stassik formal ballet lessons, and they – and Bronia, who had taught herself a sailor's dance – were allowed to take part in a children's Christmas show at Nijni Novgorod. The younger Nijinsky seems to have created something of a sensation in the *hopak*, and Foma was by no means displeased.

Gradually, as the children grew, some of the influences which were to affect Nijinsky's later career became apparent. Bronia, for instance, in her autobiography, leaves a vivid account of the great annual fair at Nijni Novgorod, during which she, Stassik and Vatsa became fascinated by the story of Petrushka, and would play out scenes from the story for hours, with herself as the dancer, Stassik as a soldier, and Vatsa as Petrushka. The maid and the valet provided their audience.

There was no question of Foma or Liota attempting to force their children into the theatre. Indeed, they were very rarely allowed to see performances. When they did so, they were entranced – though perhaps little more than most children of their age.

It was in 1897 that life began to fall apart for the family. Foma – with his fine dancer's body, his jet-black hair and beautiful hazel eyes with thick lashes – was evidently extremely attractive; and extremely susceptible. He seems to have had a number of minor affairs, from time to time, which Liota overlooked; but while he was dancing in Finland he had met a dancer called Rumiantseva and was now deeply involved with her. Bronia began to overhear constant quarrels between her parents, after her father returned from the theatre in the evenings. Soon the boys, too, knew what was going on. Vaslav responded by wild behaviour, siding passionately with his mother and being rude to his father.

In the autumn, Stassik and Bronia were infected with typhoid by their nurse (who later died of the disease). Their lives were in danger for some weeks. When they recovered, they found that their father had left home. Their mother took them to St Petersburg, then the capital of Russia, there to start a new life. She never danced again.

Liota had taken a flat at 20, Mokhovaya Street, above a piano store, and in rather distinguished company: General Kokhanovsky and the Countess Perovska, who lived in the main second and third floor apartments, kept their own carriages. The Nijinskys' flat was a small one, tucked away in a corner of the third floor; the children slept in folding beds which, during the day, made way for a dining-table and chairs. Vatsa attended school, but was not in the least given to academic studies, and indeed resorted to the age-old schoolboy custom of forging his end-of-term reports. Stassik and Bronia were still recovering from their illness, and were not to start school for some months.

Life at home was not too hard. Foma was working in Moscow, and contributed two hundred roubles a month to his family's upkeep, so they could afford one Polish servant-girl. But clearly it was time to think about Vatsa's future – and equally clearly, the only career that seemed at all promising would be in the theatre. If he could be enrolled at the Imperial Theatre School his upkeep would be paid for by the state, and his future assured – even to a state pension when he retired. Happily, Liota had a friend at court – Victor Stanislas Gillert, a Polish dancer from the Wielki Theatre who had worked at the Imperial Theatre in Moscow and had been brought to St Petersburg by the great Petipa himself, as a soloist at the Maryinsky. He now took girls' classes at the School as an assistant to the influential Cecchetti, one of the greatest teachers in the history of ballet, whose pupils were to include Pavlova, Preobrajenska, Karsavina, Kchessinskaya and Fokine. Gillert helped to prepare Vaslav for the all-important audition and entrance examination, and persuaded Cecchetti to sponsor Liota's application for an audition for her son.

On the day of the audition, Vaslav was taken to Teatralnaya Ulitza, the magnificent Theatre Street, and up to the entrance of the School under its colourful awning. Liota had planned his outfit with the greatest care: he wore a blue sailor suit with short trousers and gold buttons, cream stockings which showed off his strong legs, black leather shoes and a collar which accentuated his long neck.

First, the applicants were examined by Petipa and a colleague, who weeded out those who were obviously physically unpromising. Then came a thorough medical examination – the candidates were weighed and measured, their breathing and heart-rate considered, their hearing and sight tested. Initially there was some doubt about Vatsa's intelligence. He seemed dull and listless, unresponsive and phlegmatic. There was only one thing – he moved, and jumped, with astonishing facility, grace and energy. Eventually, the School's chief clerk appeared and read the list of those boys who were to be admitted to the School for a trial year which would lead, all being well, to their becoming permanent pupils and boarders. Vatsa's name was safely on the list. Two years later, Bronia was to join him there.

Vaslav – his childhood now effectively over – enormously enjoyed the morning ballet classes (under Sergei Legat, with whom he was a favourite), and did well in them. He was careful to behave impeccably, knowing he was on trial. Happily, his academic classes at first merely repeated work he had already done at prep. school, so it was no surprise when at the end of twelve months he was formally enrolled as a pupil. Not only Liota was delighted – so was Foma, who visited the family during the summer, while he was dancing at the St Petersburg Theatre Bouffe. His father's presence seemed to make Vaslav particularly protective of his mother, and to quieten his normally high and somewhat rebellious spirits.

At School, his now more advanced academic studies did not appeal to him, and his relationship with his fellow-pupils was bad. It was not altogether his fault. He was constantly taunted for being a Pole, for having strange, 'foreign', Mongoloid features, which earned him the nickname *Japonczek*, 'the little Jap' – a particular insult when Russia went to war with Japan. Even his accomplishments in class were mocked: 'Are you a girl, that you dance so well?' As a result he got into fights, seemed sullen

Nijinsky at school, in 1900 – the year during which he began to make serious progress as a dancer – but when he also had a serious accident which almost killed him.

and introverted, and was continually in trouble for 'bad behaviour'.

However, theatrically all went very well: he was continually chosen as an extra for theatre performances, appearing on the same stage as the great bass Chaliapin (in *Faust*), playing a mouse in *The Nutcracker* and a page in *Sleeping Beauty* and *Swan Lake*. He was awarded the Didelot Scholarship, which was a considerable financial help.

Vaslav's general high spirits won him some friends – but his great ability as a dance student equally won him some enemies; and this led, in 1901, to an unpleasant incident when during a high-jump competition in the classroom Vaslav was dared to leap over a music-stand. At the last moment it was surreptitiously raised to an almost impossible height, and then one of the students, a boy called Lukyanov, caught at Vaslav so that he crashed to the floor, unconscious. He remained in a coma for four days, and the doctors thought it unlikely that he would live. Eventually, the boy opened his eyes, and slowly recovered. He declined to implicate Lukyanov (whose family was poor, so his expulsion would have been a calamity). Three boys who did admit complicity in the dangerous prank were given black marks, and the whole matter was dropped.

Happily, no bones were broken, and at all events, though dangerous, such horse-play was not important. Class was what mattered – the vitally important early training which forms a dancer's style and confirms and advances his ability to perform the traditional steps of the ballet, forcing him to combine vigour and showmanship with neatness and apparent ease – to perform incredible feats of physical endurance without any sign of distress. Vaslav's early teachers were the Legat brothers, Sergei and Nicholas, among the principal dancers at the Maryinsky. Pavel Gerdt, the company's leading dancer, taught him mime – and laid the foundations of his impressive ability in that field. The three men were all fully aware of the boy's promise. There was no question of his not being accepted as a boarder, and in 1902 he entered Oboukhov's class, where his qualities impressed even that most critical of masters, who awarded him the highest grade he ever gave a student – eleven marks out of a possible 'perfect' twelve; other students had to be content with eight or nine.

In order to accustom themselves to stage performances, selected pupils were allowed to dance with members of the Maryinsky Company at special command performances before members of the Tsar's family, either at the Maryinsky or the exquisite little Hermitage Theatre. Sixteen couples from the school including Vaslav, danced a mazurka in *Paquita*, for instance, and he appeared also in *The Nutcracker* and *The Little Humpbacked Horse*. His success seems to have been a major factor in the speedy deterioration of Stassik's mental condition; the older boy was violently jealous, and would fly into tantrums because he, too, was not a student at the School. It was clear, however, that not only would he have been incapable of coping with that, but he was increasingly incapable of leading a normal life. A leading Russian psychiatrist concluded that it would be dangerous for him to remain at home, and he was placed, apparently permanently, in a sanatorium for the insane.

Meanwhile, in the classroom, Vaslav continued to do well at anything he liked doing – music, for instance. Though it was later asserted (by Fokine and Stravinsky, for instance) that he was a musical ignoramus, in fact he studied piano, flute, balalaika and accordian at school (his mother disapproved of the latter as vulgar!). His sister Bronia asserted that he had a remarkable ear for a score, and having heard it once could play it on the piano. On one occasion a teacher heard a piano being played, late at night, in an empty schoolroom. Investigating, he found Vaslav sitting at the keyboard playing the overture to Wagner's *Tannhäuser* – from memory. His grade was usually the highest possible, though he read music extremely slowly and indifferently.

Though academically dull, he read a great deal – Dickens and Cervantes, among other authors – and always said his favourite novel was Dostoevsky's *The Idiot*, with whose hero, Myshkin, he identified. But there is no doubt that he was decidedly antagonistic to work he did not care about, and there was a certain wildness in his behaviour – which resulted in a warning, in 1902, from the school inspector that only the excellence of his dancing prevented his dismissal.

Much of the 'wild behaviour' undoubtedly arose from an overwhelming physical vigour which simply had to be expressed in one way or another (at home,

Bronislava Nijinska, Nijinsky's sister, was herself a fine dancer and a brilliant choreographer; between 1921 and 1925 she was the sole choreographer for the Ballets Russes, and during her lifetime choreographed over 50 ballets.

it led to complaints from neighbours as Vaslav rushed madly about the corridors, one of which he had converted into a skating-rink by studious over-application of polish, and literally climbed the walls, feet pressed against one wall, hands against the other). Academically, the problem was that his performing skills led to his being frequently engaged as an extra for opera and ballet performances which kept him up until midnight almost every night, and rehearsals for which occupied much of the time when the other pupils were at lessons. The school's academic staff seem to have been incapable of realizing that this was the reason why, through exhaustion and absence from formal lessons, he inevitably fell behind his peers in examinations.

There was real trouble at the beginning of 1903. Vaslav and some friends were being taken by carriage from the school to the Maryinsky theatre, and occupied the time by using their elastic garters as slings from which they shot at passers-by with paper bullets. Someone (not, Bronia assures us, Vaslav) scored a direct hit on the top-hat of a man who unfortunately turned out to be a government official. Vaslav was persuaded to take the blame, because (with justice) his friends reckoned that he was such a good dancer the school would not expel him. They were apparently wrong; the official demanded revenge, and Vaslav was formally expelled. Tearful pleas from Liota resulted in his being re-admitted as a non-resident and allowed to attend ballet classes on condition that he was soundly beaten by a man-servant. The school further humiliated him by taking away his uniform and replacing it with a tattered second-hand one. After a month, however, he was forgiven, reinstated, and allowed the former privileges. Henceforth, he was better behaved – or perhaps simply more careful.

Until his seventeenth birthday, Vaslav's life was bounded by the life of the school, and his daily walk to and from it. On Sunday 9 January 1905, the outside world broke violently in upon him. On his way home to see his mother he was caught up in a crowd on the Nevsky Prospect and swept towards the Winter Palace where a priest, Father Gapon, was attempting to present a petition to the Tsar on behalf of his workers' union. It was Bloody Sunday – the day on which the Tsar's troops fired upon the crowd, killing, it is said, a thousand people. Cossacks charged that part of the crowd in which Vaslav was: he escaped with a wound on his forehead, and blood pouring into his eyes. The following day he had to go out with a friend, Babitch, to search for the body of Babitch's seventeen-year-old sister, who was missing. It was never found. Vaslav was too young to engage in politics (it was not then the fashion with students), but it seems most likely that it is from that date that his passion for human rights stemmed – a passion to be seen very clearly in the otherwise sad ramblings of the diary he was to write thirteen years later.

About the quality of his dancing there was, by now, no doubt. He was admitted, at an earlier age than was usual, to advanced ballet classes, where he was taught by Oboukhov and Nicholas and Sergei Legat, from whom he commanded unusual attention. Maryinsky soloists would slip into class to watch him work, and Michel Fokine, not only a teacher but a *premier danseur*, actually took the unusual step of congratulating Bronia on having such a phenomenally talented brother. Later, of course, Vaslav was to give legendary performances in *Les Sylphides*, *Carnaval*, *Spectre de la Rose*, *Schéhérazade* and *Petrushka*, all choreographed by Fokine.

Perhaps the most notable event of the school year was the annual Student Performance, which provided a shop window for the graduates hoping to be placed under contract by the Maryinsky, or failing that at least by some less notable company. For the

Nijinsky in the uniform of the Imperial Theatre School, graduating class of 1907: he received high marks for conduct, religious studies, ballet, and ballroom dancing, and only slightly lower marks for music, Russian language, history and drawing.

1905 performance, the sixteen-year-old Vaslav was chosen to partner an older graduate, Anna Fedorova, in a *pas de deux* from Pugni's *The Persian Market* choreographed by Klavdia Mikhailovna Kulichevskaya. As was usual, Oboukhov choreographed Vaslav's variation. The audience at the Maryinsky on 10 April warmly received the *adagio* of the *pas de deux*; but it was Vaslav's first jump – during which he seemed to pause for a moment in the air – that drew a gasp of delighted surprise. Almost unprecedentedly, in the middle of his variation the audience burst into applause which continued until the end, when both he and Fedorova were warmly received, but it was clearly Vaslav who had stolen the evening. (Poor Fedorova was the first, but by no means the last, partner to be overshadowed by him.) Later in the performance he danced again, in a *pas de trois* from *The Blue Danube*; even though the choreography was restrained and un-showy, the audience singled him out for special applause. Next day, a critic wrote of him, 'this student amazed everyone', and another, 'we can predict a future of laurels for this young artist'.

During 1904/5 the revolutionary American dancer Isadora Duncan actually watched one of the classes in which Vaslav took part. Her St Petersburg performances had an indirect but vital effect on Nijinsky's future career, for they inspired Fokine to try his hand at choreography.

Now that he was a senior student, Vaslav's stormy relationship with his fellows seems to have improved. He was remembered by his juniors as quiet, kindly and hardworking – at least where ballet and music were concerned – but he made no friends. Then, as later, he was a loner, and his apparent dullness of wit, a sort of reserve which was almost sullen, and which only deserted him when he began to dance, made him not only unapproachable but to an extent unattractive. His lack of accomplishment in academic subjects did not hold him back, and at the end of January, 1906, he received an unprecedented compliment: though his graduation was still eighteen months away, he was selected to perform with the Maryinsky company in a production of *Don Giovanni* celebrating the 150th anniversary of Mozart's birth, for which Fokine mounted what must have been a very odd ballet entitled 'Roses and Butterflies', which does not sound particularly Mozartian. After the performance the Imperial Ballet's director, Alexander Krupensky, personally congratulated Vaslav; at a second performance of the opera ballet, his partner was the young Anna Pavlova.

A few weeks afterwards, the School offered to release Vaslav ahead of his graduation so that he could become an Artist of the Imperial Theatre. Even though the family needed the accompanying salary of sixty-five roubles a month, Liota declined, wisely feeling that it would be too much of a strain on a seventeen-year-old to work full-time in the company.

It was not long after this that Foma Nijinsky unexpectedly appeared, excruciatingly over-dressed, at a school performance during which Vaslav danced in a Fokine *pas de deux* to Mendelssohn's *Midsummer Night's Dream* music. At first he deeply hurt Vaslav by his off-hand references to his dancing. On the following day, however, Vaslav and Bronia took Foma to the Imperial School, and showed him around. In one of the empty classrooms, the father gave his son and daughter a private exhibition of his own dancing, which they both found overwhelming in its technical brilliance – and Bronia noticed that he, too, commanded the trick of appearing to hang for a moment motionless in space. He also had an enormous jump, covering half the large classroom in one diagonal leap. Vaslav was impressed, though he later described his father's dancing as closer to acrobatics than to art.

In November 1907 Nijinsky danced in the pas classique hongrois *in* Raymonda *at a benefit performance for Maria Petipa: this was the first photograph taken of him as an Artist of the Imperial Theatre.*

Vaslav began the 1906/7 term in the pleasant knowledge that it was to mark his last year at the Imperial School. The jealousy of the other students had made life there extremely unpleasant: he associated more with the older drama students, senior to him and (it seemed) more serious-minded. By this time he was beginning to think about choreography, and devised a ballet for a children's opera, *Cinderella*, written by a young music student, Boris Vladimirovitch Asfiev (later to write the music for two major ballets, *The Flames of Paris* and *The Fountain of Bakhchisarai*). Just before Christmas he played the King of the Mice in a performance at the Maryinsky of Tchaikowsky's *The Nutcracker*.

Vaslav graduated at the Student Performance on 15 April, 1907, when he appeared in a number of pieces including 'Salanga', 'Paquita' and 'L'Animation de Gobelins' from *Le Pavillon d'Armide*, choreographed by Fokine, in which he danced with Yelizaveta Gerdt. Not only the critics were impressed. As Vaslav stood after the performance nursing a hand badly cut by the spangles on the costume of one of his partners, the great Mathilda Kchessinskaya, *prima ballerina assoluta*, former mistress of the Tsar, and lately the favourite of two Grand Dukes – the first Russian dancer to execute the formidable thirty-two *fouettés* – came up to congratulate him and announce that she intended to invite him to partner her. It was an extraordinary moment, for it meant that he would never have to appear in the *corps de ballet*; he would start his career as a *coryphé* (one rank below soloist) of the Imperial Ballet.

Oddly enough, he did not graduate top of his class – though he achieved the top grade (12) in dancing, art and music, his average grade was only 11, so he came second. Nevertheless, he was awarded not only the hundred roubles normally given to graduates, but an extra hundred – together with his diploma, a copy of the New Testament in Polish, and the complete works of Tolstoy. He then went home and wrote his formal application for a position at the Maryinsky:

'Having completed the entire course in the imperial St Petersburg Theatre School (ballet department), I have the honour to submit a most humble petition that the Office of the Imperial Theatres appoint me to active service as a dancer in the ballet troupe. Vaslav Nijinsky.'

Before his first formal appearance at the Maryinsky (where he was now officially engaged as *coryphé*, at a salary of 780 roubles a year) Nijinsky spent the summer at Krasnoe Selo, dancing with the well-known Julia Sedova at a makeshift theatre whose audience consisted chiefly of Army officers taking part in manoeuvres in the area. These performances were more important than they might seem, for among the audience were often members of the Imperial Family – the Grand Dukes and occasionally the Emperor himself. To take part in them gave Vaslav considerable social cachet.

A rare photograph of Nijinsky in practise clothes, taken while he was entertaining army officers and their wives by dancing at Krasnoe Selo during the 1907 army manoeuvres; the Emperor and members of the nobility were among audiences in the small wooden theatre.

The summer in the country was an agreeable break after the many years of school routine – though of course work continued: on three days a week, Nijinsky would travel to St Petersburg for class, then go straight to Krasnoe Selo for rehearsal and performance. A former fellow-student, Anatole Bourman (who was later to write a highly-coloured and inaccurate account of his schooldays with Vaslav) came to stay for a week, and there were picnics and excursions. Nijinsky skylarked, read, and proudly received with the other dancers the gold watch, bearing the Imperial eagle, awarded to all who appeared before the Emperor. Perhaps news of his success reached his father, still touring with his own company. At all events at the end of the summer a letter arrived inviting the boy to come to Nijny-Novgorod to visit him. He was not inclined to accept

– he always took his mother's side, and was extremely reserved in his attitude to Foma. However, Liota insisted that he should go.

The visit was not a success. Tactlessly, Thomas attempted to introduce his partner and mistress, Rumiantseva, and spoke of their child. Vaslav took exception to this and immediately walked out. He and his father never met again. And from that moment, the family received no more money from Foma; he did not even attend Bronia's graduation from the Imperial School.

When the Maryinsky season began in September 1907, the future looked brighter than the Nijinskys could have hoped only a year or so preivously. Only the continued incarceration of Stassik struck a note of sadness; otherwise all was well –even, for the first time, financially, for Vaslav was now paid sixty-five roubles a month, and had saved a thousand roubles during the summer; he was also able to make a hundred roubles an hour teaching social dance to the two children of a rich St Petersburg miller. Bronia was now a member of the company, with an income of her own. Liota was able to take a decent-sized flat on Torgovaya Ulitza, and the family's standard of living rose accordingly.

By now, Vaslav was beginning to lose some of his shyness, and to flirt with one or two of the girls in the company – in fact, he was out of favour with Nicholas Legat, who took company class, because of a flirtation with a young dancer called Antonina Tchumakova with whom Legat was in love (and who he later married). Vaslav dropped another girl-friend when she expressed her admiration of Isadora Duncan, of whose free style of dancing he was not an admirer, and learned a final lesson when, after announcing his intention of marrying Maria Gorshkova, he found that what she really wanted was to ride to her own success on the back of his.

His brilliant graduation performance and accounts of his summer season at Krasnoe Selo stood him in good stead during his first season at the Maryinsky. He danced in several *pas de deux*, appearing first with Sedova, later with Lydia Kyasht (who in the following year was to make an enormous success at the Empire Theatre in London, and eventually settled in England), and finally with Karsavina. As she had promised, the great Kchessinskaya asked for him to partner her in *La Fille Mal Gardée* and in a *divertissement* for the farewell performance for Maria Petipa. He is not generally associated with light, humorous roles, but in *Fille* his humour and inventiveness were much admired, as was his love-play with Kchessinskaya. He was becoming extremely well-known to the balletomanes of St Petersburg, and, more gradually, to the men who were to be involved in his short, brilliant career.

One day, Fokine brought Alexandre Benois to the practice-room in Theatre Street. A Russian designer and art historian, Benois had some years earlier suggested to the director of the Maryinsky an idea for a ballet based on a story by Theophile Gautier, to be called *Le Pavillon d'Armide* (a scene from which Nijinsky had danced at his graduation). Now a full production had been approved, and Fokine was to choreograph the complete work to a score by Nicholas Tcherapnine, with Benois to design it. He was fascinated by the scene in the dancers' studio, in which everyone moved so freely and easily, in such complete contrast to the stiff formality of their stage appearances. Among the boys of the School stood an older boy who was presented to Benois as the dancer who would play the part of Armida's slave – which was just as well, Benois thought, for as a personality he was almost completely colourless – 'more like a shop-assistant than a fairy-tale hero'.

There were various problems during rehearsals

for the ballet: for some reason the Maryinsky's Director took against it, then Kchessinskaya, who had been going to dance Armida, resigned, and Pavlova took over. But the first performance, on 25 November 1907, was a triumph – the first of many ballets in which Nijinsky, Benois and Fokine were to be involved together. Vaslav, though in a minor role, had an important variation including four leaps which took him right across the vast Maryinsky stage, and a set of double *pirouettes* in the air, landing on one foot and moving diagonally, finishing with a triple *pirouette*.

Three days later, Nijinsky danced, with Lydia Kyasht, the 'Bluebird' *pas de deux* from Act III of *The Sleeping Beauty*. It was perhaps the most astonishing display of his art which had yet been seen, a soaring solo in which he really seemed to fly, his hands fluttering so swiftly that they were blurred like trembling wings. It was a performance which was to continue to astound audiences, however often it was repeated. The Maryinsky audience, which had seen the solo danced a hundred times by many dancers, went mad with enthusiasm. This was not the tribute of fashionable ignoramuses – Maryinsky audiences really knew about the ballet – and knew this particular *pas de deux* as well as the dancers who performed it. They recognized genius when they saw it.

A tiny incident in the history of the ballet occurred at Christmas, 1907: Nijinsky was unable to dance with Pavlova because of a bad cold, and instead of performing with another partner she presented a new solo choreographed for her by Fokine to the music of 'The Swan' by Saint-Saëns – the first appearance of her most famous piece.

By his twentieth year, Nijinsky, while not in any sense a 'star', was attracting attention as one of the most promising young members of the company. It was in one special sense a dangerous (or, depending on how one looked at it, a promising) situation. While in Russia the ballet never became the sort of slave-market to be found at the Paris Opéra – virtually, a display-case for young dancing prostitutes available to members of the Jockey Club – cases in which young members of the Maryinsky *corps* attached themselves to rich admirers were not unknown; and, contrary to the practice in Paris, it was an accepted fact that just as some of the girls came under the protection of impressive members of the aristocracy, so some male dancers also engaged in affairs with 'protectors'.

According to the Russian critic and biographer of Nijinsky, Vera Krasovskaya, it was after the first performance of *Pavillon d'Armide* that a note was passed to Vaslav in his dressing-room. It read, 'I would like to make your acquaintance. Would you agree to celebrate your success in a restaurant? My friends and I will be waiting for you at the stage door. Lvov.' Prince Pavel Dmitrievitch Lvov was a good looking thirty-year-old aristocrat, a patron of sport, the first man in St Petersburg to own a motor car – indeed, he owned two, a sedan and a four-seater coupé in which he took Nijinsky and Bronia to bicycle races and horse shows. Besides sport, he was interested in all the arts, and particularly in Nijinsky. He began to take him to fashionable restaurants and nightclubs (at one of which the black American tap-dancer Claude Hopkins must have reminded Vaslav of Johnson and Johnson) and also to concerts: every Sunday they would go to hear Rachmaninov or Rimsky-Korsakov play their own music, or to hear the spectacular pianist Josef Hoffman.

Vaslav enjoyed himself enormously. He had always – even before he could really afford it – been something of a dandy, and now spent quite a lot of money on fine clothes – in particular, on a really well-cut dinner jacket. He began to feel at home in the kind of society in which Lvov moved, at his elegant home in Bolshaya Morskaya Ulitza, where every room seemed like a museum, rich with *objets d'art*, and where Vaslav was encouraged to play on the very piano at which Hoffman had performed. We can only guess at Vaslav's sexual response to what was obviously a pick-up. Affairs between men were at that time entirely acceptable in St Petersburg, so there would have been no social disapproval. Vaslav, though naive, must have known what was going on and certainly did not discourage Lvov's attentions; his diary, written years later, suggests that he actually fell in love with him.

There was inevitably a great deal of gossip about them, about Vaslav's increasingly expensive wardrobe, about the handsome grand piano he had acquired. His colleagues were on the whole happy to spread and augment the rumours, for there was a very great deal of jealousy of his increasing success, and while such behaviour was not unknown, it was not positively approved of. Maria Gorshkova apparently put it about that he was incapable of loving a woman. Zina Puyman, another member of the company, invited Bronia to tea especially to warn her of the insinuations which were being made about her brother's friendship with Prince Lvov.

But whatever the true circumstances of their relationship, there is no doubt that the Prince was an excellent influence, and of considerable practical help. He introduced the young dancer to musicians and painters, entertained him (and Bronia) regally, paid a hundred roubles a month for extra lessons with Cecchetti and encouraged his friends to engage Vaslav as a teacher of social dance, thus considerably enhancing his income.

In the meantime, work continued, and Nijinsky was preparing for a visit to Paris, where he was to appear with Kchessinskaya at the Opéra.

But the Paris début had to wait, for, embarrassingly Nijinsky now went down with venereal disease, apparently as the result of a casual affair with a female prostitute (he may have responded to some of his colleagues' taunts, daring him to 'prove himself a man'). Lvov called in a specialist to treat him, loaned him his valet to care for him, and when he had recovered carried him off to spend the summer of 1908 at his summer villa on an island near Novaya Derevnia at Sestroretzk, where he relaxed, played tennis, and talked about art or, at least, was lectured on it.

Back in St Petersburg the family moved, in the summer of 1908, into a comfortable apartment at 13, Bolshaya Koniushennaya – and even acquired a telephone. Nijinsky now had a study as well as a bedroom, and Prince Lvov furnished the rooms for him. Bronia recalled evenings spent in those rooms, while her brother sat at the Bluthner grand piano playing, sometimes his own compositions.

Another figure, however, now stepped upon the stage: that of Sergei Pavlovich Diaghilev. Bourman claims that it was Lvov who introduced Vaslav to the man who was to make him world-famous; at all events, by 1909 they were often to be seen together. Vaslav told Bronia that the older man was introducing him to some fascinating friends: it would be nice if she were able to meet them too, but somehow there seemed never to be any women at Diaghilev's apartment. . . .

Diaghilev was born in Novgorod in 1872, the son of an officer in the Imperial Guard whose musical interests had brought him the friendship of Tchaikowsky and Mussorgsky. After a conventional education, Diaghilev went to St Petersburg in 1890 to study law at the University, and also to take singing and musical composition at the Conservatory. Before his studies were complete he had already begun to contribute art criticism to a daily newspaper, and was one of a group of theatre and art enthusiasts which included Benois and Leon Bakst, who was to design so many ballets for him.

Sergei Pavlovitch Diaghilev (1872-1929), the ballet's greatest impresario. His presentation of a season of ballet in Paris in 1909 marked the beginning of a revolution in Western art; Nijinsky was only one of the great dancers he presented – among the others, Pavlova, Karsavina, Lopokova, Massine, Sokolova, Dolin, Markova. His choreographers included Fokine, Nijinska, Balanchine; his artists, Benois, Bakst, Picasso, Matisse, Derain, Marie Laurencin; his composers, Poulenc, Auric, Satie.

After travelling in Europe with his cousin Dmitri Filosofov, studying pictures and antiques and listening to the new music, Diaghilev founded a luxurious art magazine, *Mir Isskustva – The World of Art*, backed by a philanthropic Moscow millionaire. Running from 1899 until 1904, it was undoubtedly a very impressive publication, printing essays by every important Russian critic of its time.

During the year in which *The World of Art* was founded, Diaghilev became for the first time involved with the theatre. A friend of his, Prince Sergei Volkonsky, became Director of the Maryinsky and engaged Diaghilev as an assistant with special responsibility for the production of the theatre's *Annals*, a yearbook which was formerly as dull and stolid as any annual report, but which Diaghilev characteristically turned into a wonderfully illustrated coffee-table book which received the admiration even of the Tsar.

That success seems rather to have gone to his head. Together with Filosofov, Benois and Bakst, he began in 1901 to plan a new production of Delibes' ballet *Sylvia*, with the Legat brothers and Olga Preobrajenskaya (one of the greatest dancers of the Imperial Ballet) in the leading roles. Unfortunately, some of Volkonsky's older colleagues became violently jealous of the young group of artists which seemed to be plotting some kind of takeover. Volkonsky at first tried to heal the breach by persuading Diaghilev at least to allow the names of some of his seniors to appear on the programme of the ballet. Diaghilev took a superior attitude and refused, threatening to throw up the editing of the *Annals*. Two days later he opened the Government gazette to read that he had been dismissed from his position at the theatre under an article which was normally only invoked in cases of extremely disreputable behaviour.

This was a blow to his pride; but his energies

were too irrepressible to allow him time to sulk. He organized a series of annual *World of Art* exhibitions, presenting in all sixteen shows in St Petersburg, Moscow, Berlin, Cologne, Düsseldorf, Darmstadt and Venice. He spent 1904 travelling around Russia seeking out unfamiliar and forgotten portraits of members of the great Russian families for his most notable achievement to date – the enormous 1905 exhibition of Russian Historical Portraits; three thousand pictures hung in the Tauride Palace, with, at its centre, a winter garden designed by Bakst. The Tsar opened the exhibition, walking through it for two hours with many members of his family.

Then, in 1906, Diaghilev seriously set his sights on taking Russian art and artists to the West. First came the exhibition of Russian painters in the Petit Palais in Paris, where he showed work ranging from fifteenth century icons and seventeenth and eighteenth century portraits to the most recent work of Benois, Bakst, Serov, Dobujinsky, Roerich and Larianov. In May 1907, five concerts of Russian music at the Paris Opéra – Rimsky-Korsakov, Rachmaninov and Glazunov conducted their own work, and the great Chaliapin sang for the first time in the city. The magnificent bass almost caused a riot, so enthusiastic were the audiences who heard him, and Diaghilev determined to bring him back to Paris in 1908 – and in a role in which he considered him to be at his best (though it had never been popular in St Petersburg), Mussorgsky's *Boris Godunov*. As was so often the case, his instinct was right: despite great difficulties at the Opéra, where there were insufficient rehearsals and the sets were only in position an hour or so before the first performance, the opera stunned all who heard it. Diaghilev returned home in triumph. And it was now, when the West seemed to offer magnificent opportunities to a lively impresario, that he met Nijinsky. He was thirty-four, the dancer seventeen.

Right *Nijinsky first danced with Anna Pavlova in 1906, and a year later partnered her in* Le Pavillon d'Armide, *in which the choreographer Michel Fokine and his designer Alexandre Benois brought to life a Gobelins tapestry.*

He had seen Vaslav on stage in *Le Pavillon d'Armide* and in a version of Michel Fokine's *Chopiniana* (a suite of dances to music by Chopin in which Vaslav had appeared as a dreaming poet in black velvet, dancing with Pavlova, Karsavina and Preobrajenskaya). No doubt he was as impressed by his stage personality and technique as other St Petersburg balletomanes. But there was another ingredient in his admiration. Diaghilev was a homosexual whose love was always to be directed at young men of artistic sensitivity – his cousin Filosofov seems to have been his first lover – or of great potential. Clearly, Nijinsky possessed these attributes in the greatest degree. Vaslav records in his diary that on their first evening alone, 'I allowed him to make love to me. I trembled like a leaf.'

Ridiculously, Nijinsky also asserted that he became Diaghilev's lover because otherwise he and his mother would have died of hunger. This, of course, is nonsense; he was an established soloist with every prospect of making a handsome income for the rest of his dancing life, and afterwards would have received a state pension. One can only guess at the truth: it seems most likely that Diaghilev, with his forceful, persuasive personality, simply swept the young man, whose experience of life was so slender, off his feet. And no doubt, knowing of Diaghilev's importance and influence in the world of the arts, there was an element of ingratiation in Nijinsky's reaction to the older man's approaches. It would be silly to imagine that a young man in Nijinsky's position would not be likely to 'seek his luck,' as he himself put it. (The circumstances were mirrored sixteen years later when Diaghilev engaged the English dancer Anton Dolin: when Dolin took the train from the Gare de Lyon for Monte Carlo, he found his belongings had been moved from his own single compartment to Diaghilev's double-berth sleeper. 'I knew perfectly well what was expected of me,' he said, many years later. Having been seduced as a boy, by a priest in the confessional, he probably coped with the situation with more equanimity than Vaslav).

There is one other element which perhaps explains Nijinsky's immediate capitulation. Whatever his true sexual nature (and it is clear that he was bisexual rather than entirely homosexual), it certainly seems to be true that his first heterosexual experience was catastrophic: the prostitute who infected him had also been unsympathetic and in some way intimidating. A more tender approach from a man almost old enough to be the father Vaslav, in his late childhood and early youth, had lacked, must have seemed infinitely safer and more attractive. There was also the cachet of being seen continually in the company of one of the most exciting and influential men in the world of Russian art, and there was Diaghilev's generosity – during the early days of their friendship he gave Vaslav a complete set of *Mir Isskustva* and of the catalogues of all his art exhibitions.

At all events, in one way and another the autumn of 1908 was a turning-point in Nijinsky's life. Already, Diaghilev's thoughts were turning towards the possibility of a ballet season in Paris next year – a season which was to make his new protégé the sensation of the city, and eventually of the Western world.

CHAPTER II

Wonder of Wonders 1908–1909

Throughout the winter of 1908/9 Nijinsky was often at Diaghilev's flat on the Fontanka Quay, opposite the Sheremetiev Palace, when the choreographer and his associates met to plan the 1909 Paris season of opera and ballet. Alexandre Benois and Leon Bakst were of course present, with the painters Nicholas Roerich, Alexander Golovine and Konstantin Korovine; the composers Glazunov and Nicholas Tcherepnin, the *réqisseurs* Vsevolod Meyerhold and Alexander Sanine, Prince Argutinsky-Dolgorukov and other balletomanes. Bronia suggests that the company seriously inhibited him: while he had his own opinions about the ballet and its future, at this time at least he was extremely wary of expressing them in the company of much more experienced men, most of whom were also immeasurably his social superiors.

Michel Fokine, a soloist at the Maryinsky and an ambitious young choreographer, was told to rehearse *Le Pavillon d'Armide* and *Les Sylphides* (as Diaghilev wanted to call the new, extended version of *Chopiniana*). He had been pressing the claims of *Une Nuit d'Egypte*, originally staged for a children's matinée in March 1908 to music by Anton Stepanovich Arensky – Pavlova and Paul Gerdt, the veteran dancer and teacher, had appeared in it together with Nijinsky, who had partnered Preobrajenskaya in a slave dance. But Diaghilev thought the score very weak for sophisticated Paris. On the other hand, the idea of a ballet on Egyptian themes was an original and lively one, and finally he was persuaded, and asked Fokine to re-choreograph it as *Cléopâtre*, dropping Arensky's overture and replac-

Left *Those who claim that Nijinsky had no sense of humour might like to study the wicked gleam in his eye in this pose from* Le Festin, *which suggests that he took the ballet – and himself – less seriously than one might have expected.*

ing it by one from an opera by Alexander Taneyev, and inserting music by several other composers including Rimsky-Korsakov, Glinka, Glazunov and Mussorgsky. Rather grimly, Fokine agreed to try to make something of the hotch-potch, only insisting that the part of Cleopatra should be played by his young pupil Ida Rubenstein, an actress whose appearance as Oscar Wilde's *Salomé* had been prevented after the Russian censor had attended the dress rehearsal.

Fokine had already started work on the choreography for the Polovtsian Dances in Borodin's *Prince Igor*, and with *Cléopâtre* had as much work as he could cope with. Diaghilev had the operatic part of the Paris season to plan: Glinka's *Russlan and Ludmilla*, *Prince Igor*, *Boris* and Rimsky-Korsakov's *The Maid of Pskov*. There was no time to prepare another original ballet; so they devised a suite of dances to be called *Le Festin*, consisting of pieces from operas and ballets already in the repertory of the Maryinsky and Moscow Imperial Theatres – among them the 'Bluebird' *pas de deux* from Petipa's *The Sleeping Beauty*, rather oddly renamed 'Fire Bird', to be danced by Karsavina and Nijinsky, and a *Grand Pas Classique Hongrois* from Glazunov's *Raymonda*, in which Vaslav and his sister Bronia were to appear.

And which dancers were to go to Paris? Pavlova, Karsavina and Nijinsky were obvious choices to support the distinguished Kchessinskaya. Ida Rubenstein was a somewhat sensational choice – but Fokine was persuasive, and Diaghilev, never being afraid of sensationalism, overruled objections about a non-professional being included in the company. Finally, he engaged the *corps* before going off to Paris early in 1909 to complete arrangements for the season.

The intrigue and plotting among the St Petersburg dancers was considerable. No one doubted, from the

Right *Her whole body covered with light turquoise-green, Ida Rubenstein created the title role in* Cléopâtra *(1909); carried on stage in a sarcophagus resting on a catafalque, she was undressed by her slaves, and sat half-naked (in Nijinska's words) with Nijinsky crouching low at her feet 'like a black panther, her hand adorned with jewels resting on his black head.' The ballet was perhaps most important for Bakst's immensely influential décor.*

beginning, that Nijinsky would be a leading member of the Paris group, and that presumably Bronia would also be going. Vaslav was by now passionately protective of his younger sister and would rush to her defence if she was criticised, or if he thought she was slighted. When her name was not on Diaghilev's first list, Vaslav intervened to assure her a position in the company – she was never a particularly remarkable dancer (though she was to become a remarkable choreographer). As a result, her friends crowded around her, dropping hints that she might persuade her brother to put their names forward; some of Vaslav's enemies became, suddenly, rather attached to him.

While Diaghilev was away, his friend and patron the Grand Duke Vladimir Alexandrovitch, who had promised a hundred-thousand-rouble subsidy for the Paris season, died, and the subsidy was withdrawn – perhaps because of an intrigue on the part of Kchessinskaya, who had decided not to appear because the part she had been offered in *Le Pavillon d'Armide* was not sufficiently important. Never to be deterred by lack of money, Diaghilev engaged in various machinations to save the season. Gabriel Astruc, who had managed the previous Paris visit, turned out to have a persuasive way with various French financiers, and managed to raise the necessary funds. Diaghilev returned to St Petersburg in time to attend, on 2 April 1909, the very first rehearsal of his company – at the Hermitage Theatre, which had been placed at his disposal (one advantage of this was that during a suitable break in the proceedings court footmen would process into the auditorium with tea and chocolate for the dancers). After only a few days, alas, the order came through that the theatre was no longer available and the dancers, many of them in practice clothes, crossed the city in a fleet of taxis to the little German club near the Ekaterina Canal, which Diaghilev rented for the remaining rehearsals.

It was at this time that Diaghilev was first noticed by other members of the company to be keeping an almost proprietorial eye on Nijinsky, either personally or through his faithful valet Vassili. Nijinsky, however, let nothing interfere with his work. Even Fokine, in his notably splenetic autobiography of 1961, remembered that Vaslav was wonderfully quick at catching every detail of any movement shown him, and at intuitively performing precisely what the choreographer wanted. This was specially valuable in the re-working of *Chopiniana* as *Les Sylphides*, generally regarded as the first entirely abstract ballet.

Its history is interesting: Fokine's first sketches, mounted to the Glazunov orchestrations of four Chopin pieces (plus one extra piece the composer arranged at the choreographer's request), were staged at a charity performance in February, 1907 (see page 44) as *Chopiniana.* They were a *polonaise, nocturne, mazurka, tarantella* and *valse* – the latter danced by Pavlova in a costume designed by Bakst after an 1840 lithograph of Marie Taglioni in the earlier ballet *La Sylphide*. The dances were revived in 1907 as *Danses sur la Musique de Chopin*, and in 1909 were performed again at the Maryinsky, when Vaslav and Pavlova danced; Bronia always considered that it was at that revival that the set of dances really became the ballet *Les Sylphides*, perhaps the most popular ballet of its time.

The male role in particular was completely different from that expected by an audience: there was no showing off, no double turns or spectacular leaps. Instead the dancer had to be aware only of the sylphs around him, to seem to be 'longing and reaching toward some fantastic world'. Far from being in any way annoyed at not being able to show off his technical skill, Nijinsky immediately understood what Fokine wanted, and entered into the spirit of the piece.

Fokine's Les Sylphides, *one of the best-known and most popular of all ballets, originated at a charity performance in 1907 as* Chopiniana, *a suite of dances to the music of Chopin. In it Pavlova danced a pas de deux with Mikhail Oboukhov, in which she wore a long white tutu from the 1832 ballet* La Sylphide; *the ballet we know was derived from this dance. Right, the opening tableau.*

He had other opportunities for technical feats. Into *Le Pavillon d'Armide*, for instance, Fokine had inserted a special solo for Nijinsky – indeed, had insisted to the librettist, Benois, that the part of Armida's favourite slave should be much enlarged, to make provison for his talents. This, in the first version of the ballet, opened with a standing leap without any preparation and with the feet held together – a difficult task which Nijinsky executed with the greatest ease, grace and simplicity, and apparently without the slightest effort.

Rumours of a special relationship between Diaghilev and Nijinsky were strengthened when the two set off for Paris well before the rest of the company. Not long after they left St Petersburg, Prince Lvov called on Liota and with tears in his eyes told her that Diaghilev had informed him that Nijinsky now no longer required his friendship or support, and that if he really wished the dancer well he would not continue to force his attentions on him. Lvov not only accepted this, but actually gave the impresario a considerable sum of money towards the expenses of the Paris season. No wonder that for the rest of his life Vaslav continued to speak well of him.

Liota and Bronia followed Vaslav to Paris with the rest of the company, which was placed in various small hotels: Nijinsky had at first been placed in the Hôtel Daunou, near the Avenue de l'Opéra, but was now with Diaghilev (and the impresario's secretary and perhaps by now only former lover, Alexis Mavrine) at the Hôtel de Hollande, in the Rue de la Paix; Karsavina was at the Hôtel Normandie, off the Avenue de l'Opéra; and Liota and Bronia, with other dancers, were in the Boulevard St Michel, just across

Nijinsky as a Spanish gypsy in a dance from the 1846 ballet Paquita*; this photograph was probably taken in 1907/8, either at the time of his graduation performance at the Maryinsky Theatre, or shortly afterwards, when he performed (with Lydia Kyasht) excerpts from that ballet during his first month as an Artist of the Imperial Theatre.*

Les Sylphides *was first seen in Paris on 4 June 1909, with Nijinsky and Karsavina; now that it has become a classic we forget how revolutionary it must have seemed then – the first abstract ballet.*

the river from the Théâtre du Châtelet, where the season was to take place. After rehearsals, Vaslav would invariably go around to his mother's small room, where she would have tea ready, with pastries, ham, cheese and pâté de fois gras.

There were two weeks for final rehearsals and preparations, including the organization of the machinery of publicity – something at which Diaghilev was never less than brilliant. On this occasion, there was little need for it, since by 10 May most tickets had already been sold and extra performances announced. Meanwhile, despite his customary lack of money, Diaghilev had ordered the redecoration of the theatre and the removal of five rows of stalls to accommodate the large orchestra. The Châtelet was in chaos. Stage rehearsals took place amid a constant din of sawing and hammering which drove Fokine to distraction. Diaghilev at one point ordered all the pit seats to be ripped up and replaced by boxes: Fokine protested; the order was countermanded. Each morning the chaos would be interrupted while trestle tables were set up on stage and laden with food and coffee; the dancers, with Diaghilev and Fokine, would cluster around for an informal lunch. Then the opera company arrived and insisted on a share of the time on stage, so the dancers were packed off to a hot, windowless attic.

It did not matter too much, for there was no need for intense rehearsal: all the dances planned for the season were familiar – all that was needed was to work on the tempi with the orchestra and conductor. Meanwhile, of course, ordinary classes continued – the daily practice which maintains and strengthens the dancer's technique.

Nijinsky scarcely ever joined the general class, preferring to work alone. He would do this for between forty-five and fifty minutes each day, performing all the usual ballet exercises, but at a quicker tempo than most ballet-masters would have set, so that his sister considered that within a shorter period than that of a conventional class, he used as much energy as a normal dancer would expend in three hours.

He did not concern himself a great deal with the formal five ballet positions, concentrating on developing strength and speed of movement. He would dance every step full out while practising, building up reserves of strength which enabled him to make those same movements seem effortless when he was on stage. Muscularly, he was extremely strong, but there were limitations to his movements: because of the almost abnormal development of his thigh muscles, he could not, for instance, raise his legs higher than ninety degrees. (Some photographs clearly reveal his huge thigh muscles, which were such that his tailor had to adjust the trousers of his suits so that they fitted properly.)

Practising jumps, he would seem to land not so much on the balls of his feet as on his toes, which were unusually strong, and enabled him to continue to jump apparently without further preparation – he did not need to take the *pliés* necessary to other dancers. He seemed to take *pirouettes* without any preparation at all, progressing from five to seven, then nine, then twelve or even sixteen, again apparently effortlessly.

He also used gymnastic techniques to increase his strength; while still at school, he would borrow dumb-bells and weights and bring them home to work with them during weekends. Bronia records that while still in his teens, he could lift 32 kg with one arm.

One or two favoured journalists were allowed to watch rehearsals and described the chaos and the dancers who endured it: the 'dark, slender girl with almond eyes and an ivory complexion who evokes dreams of the gorgeous East' (Vera Karalli, *prima ballerina* of the Moscow Bolshoi Theatre), 'the

Valentin Svetlov's famous poster for the Ballets Russes 1909 season, starring Anna Pavlova.

elusive, thoughtful beauty who seems wafted by infinite grace' (Karsavina), and 'the extraordinary Nijinsky, a kind of modern Vestris (who had been for thirty-six years *premier danseur* at the Paris Opéra, and was said 'on one leg to do what erst no mortal could achieve on two'), but whose dazzling technique is allied to a plastic feeling and a distinction of gesture which are certainly unequalled elsewhere'.

Diaghilev also invited various favoured members of Parisian artistic society to watch his dancers at work. Bronia noticed, for instance, a strange young man in fashionable clothes who spent a lot of time with Vaslav, and who seemed to be wearing rouge and lipstick. He was, Vaslav explained, an up-and-coming young poet, Jean Cocteau, and make-up was *de rigueur* in the circles in which he moved.

The company was now prepared. *Le Figaro* was printing a series of thumb-nail sketches of the dancers. All round the city appeared Sorel's now famous charcoal sketch of Pavlova which was used on the company's first poster. On 16 May the orchestra arrived from Moscow (except for one oboeist, who had got out at Smolensk by mistake). And two days later the theatre doors opened at eight o'clock and the audience filed in for the *répétition générale* or public dress rehearsal (a 'preview', as we would now call it).

Before a single note of music sounded, the audience examined itself and saw a work of art. Gabriel Astruc, Diaghilev's press manager, had papered the house with the most distinguished men and women in the city. The French Foreign Minister and the Russian Ambassador shared the centre box, four other government ministers nearby. The world of fashion was represented by prominent hostesses, and the world of art by – among others – Daudet, Forain, Rodin, Lalo, Fauré, Saint-Saëns, Ravel and Pascal. Isadora Duncan was there, with Carlotta Zambelli (the current star of the Opera). Chaliapin, soon himself to appear on stage, was also in the audience, as were representatives of the Opéra, the Opéra Comique, the Monte Carlo Opera and the Metropolitan Opera House, New York – and indeed of the music-hall, including the great Yvette Guilbert, once drawn by Toulouse-Lautrec. Finally, to provide a sort of necklace right around the dress-circle of the theatre, Astruc had had the brilliant idea of sending tickets to the most beautiful girls from the Opéra and the Comédie-Française.

Backstage was the controlled despair of the moments before the raising of the curtain. The evening was to open with *Le Pavillon d'Armide*, with Karalli as Armida and Nijinsky as the Favourite Slave. By now in his dressing-room, where the sticks of grease-paint lay in careful rows on the dressing-table, he was ready. He had arrived at the theatre an hour earlier, put on his practice clothes, and at the back of the stage put himself through the series of

Alexandre Benois (1870–1960), for some time Artistic Director of the Ballets Russes, designed five ballets for Diaghilev, the earliest of which was Le Pavillon d'Armide, *a fantasy ballet he himself devised: it opened in a baroque pavilion with tall windows between which stood a giant ormolu clock with two dancers impersonating Time and Love; the costumes were of the late Louis XIV period.*

exercises with which all dancers must warm up before a performance. Then he had washed and made up: this took half an hour. Then on with the costume, designed of course by Benois – and the moment came when Vaslav began to become the character the audience would see on stage:

'He gradually began to change into another being, the one he saw in the mirror. He became reincarnated and actually *entered into* his new existence as an exceptionally attractive and poetical personality. The fact that Nijinsky's metamorphosis was predominantly subconscious is in my opinion the very proof of his genius. Only a genius – that is to say, a phenomenon that has no adequate natural explanation – could incarnate the choreographic essence of the rococo period as did Nijinsky in *Le Pavillon d'Armide* – especially in the Paris version of my ballet.'

Three raps behind the curtain signalled the start of the performance; Tcherepnine lifted his baton for the first bars of the score, and the curtain rose.

The music of *Le Pavillon d'Armide* has not been performed for many years, and the ballet has not been seen for even longer. The plot concerns a young nobleman, visiting an old mansion, who falls in love with a beautiful enchantress who emerges from a Gobelin tapestry. At the ballet's centre is a scene in a woodland clearing during which a series of *divertissements* is danced – and it was this scene which was to make a lasting impression on the Paris audience.

Into Benois' forest glade came Karsavina and Alexandre Baldina, as Armida's two confidantes, dressed in yellow and gold, followed by Nijinsky as the Favourite Slave, in a white, yellow and silver costume embellished with festoons of silk, lace ruffles and ermine, with an ornate, heavy top-coat, wired skirt or *tonnelet* (based on the parade armour which had become almost a uniform for male dancers in the eighteenth century) and knee-breeches

In Le Pavillon d'Armide, *in which the figures of a Gobelin tapestry come to life, Nijinsky appeared as the Favourite Slave of the Princess Armida; it was a part specially conceived to show off his dancing, and the elegance of his movements, his high jumps and impeccable* pirouettes, *provoked cheering at the end of his solo on the ballet's first performance in Paris.*

with garters, a jewelled choker around his neck, and on his head a white silk turban with an ostrich-feather. The three began to dance: and at that moment the audience recognized a quality which had not been seen in Paris within living memory. An excited murmur was heard; and at the end, when the two women made their exit, there was a gasp as Nijinsky ran towards the wings and then rose into an extended parabola which took him from the stage in a curve which seemed as though it must continue well beyond the limits of the theatre. The gasp turned into a roar of applause. With that one leap, which was not part of the choreography and was performed on the spur of the moment, Nijinsky constructed his own legend.

But of course the ballet did not end there. A moment later Vaslav reappeared for his solo, with more leaps and *pirouettes*, interspersed with the most graceful movements of the arms and inclinations of the body. Almost every critic describing him spoke of his soaring like a bird, apparently free of the confines of gravity, of the confines of what had been previously thought to be the technique of the dance. He later recalled that throughout his solo he was conscious of a strange, gradually increasing noise in the auditorium; at first he thought it was the sound of disapproval, or perhaps even of consternation – had some disaster occurred? But the sound was one of astonishment and appreciation, and once more swelled into applause and cheering as he left the stage.

Nijinsky as the Favourite Slave of Princess Armida in Le Pavillon d'Armide.

Le Pavillon d'Armide had other delights to offer, of course – the delicious Karsavina, and the strange excitement of Russian character-dancing, which Parisian audiences had never seen before. There were many curtain-calls. And then came *Prince Igor*. Bare of Benois' extravagant designs, the Polovtsian Dances were staged against an empty sky across which rose trails of smoke from the tents of the Polovtsi (a design by Nicholas Roerich). The opera chorus set the scene for the wild and frenzied dances of the warriors, led by Adolph Bolm, then the languid, intensely erotic dances of the women, with Sophie Feodorova leading them. Another roar of applause; more curtain-calls. By this time the audience was in a state of delirium. The pass-doors from the auditorium were broken down and a crowd invaded the stage. Nijinsky and Karsavina, warming-up for the final ballet, were conscious of curious onlookers pressing in on them as they rehearsed their lifts.

Le Festin was no less successful than the preceding ballets; as part of it, Karsavina and Nijinsky danced the Tchaikowsky/Petipa 'Bluebird' variation. Originally, Diaghilev had announced a new ballet – *L'Oiseau de Feu* – for the season, choreographed to music by Liadov; when he found that Liadov had not even begun the score, he speedily inserted the 'Bluebird' *pas de deux* into *Le Festin*, re-naming it *L'Oiseau de Feu*. It was danced third in the series of *divertissements*, and once more amazed the audience. Bakst's costume designs (his first to be seen in the West) had surprisingly turned Karsavina into the bird, while Nijinsky became a bejewelled and turbanned prince. (It may have been these designs which led to a persistent confusion in the West about this *pas de deux*; there always seems to be some doubt about who is bird and who human.)

This is one of Petipa's most brilliant and effective *pas de deux*, and when well performed remains in the memory as long as anything in *The Sleeping Beauty*. In this case the effect made by Nijinsky and the luminous Karsavina was never forgotten by anyone who saw that first Paris programme. Bakst had dressed Nijinsky in a lime-green, mustard and gold costume, the heavy quilted tunic sewn with pearls and topazes. Though obviously human, Nijinsky still performed the steps and movements Petipa had

The designs of the Russian artist Leon Bakst (1866–1924) played an enormously important part in the early success of the Ballets Russes, not only through his costume designs (shown here, Nijinsky's costume for Le Festin*) but in décor and in make-up. Nijinska said he inspired all the dancers, understanding every detail of interpretation.*

invented for the Bluebird (he had learned them from Enrico Cecchetti, the first Bluebird, who had been taught them by the choreographer). His hands, for instance, still fluttered like the bird's wings – and Massine, who was to see him dance the part some years later, recalled that 'to convey the quivering motion of the bird's wings he fluttered his hands at such a dazzling speed that they seemed to have exactly the pulsating action of humming-birds. I learned later that he had done this by doubling the rate of his wrist movements.'

The Paris audiences failed to notice the ludicrous notion of a bird dressed as a man. By now, the onlookers were past anything less than uncritical adulation. It was as if, one of Diaghilev's party said, their seats were on fire. The *Danse Caucasienne* which formed the finale to *Le Festin* raised them to hysteria: again, Vaslav transformed himself – this time from the slender, boyish figure of the Prince into the virile, proud, provocative captain of the Lezgins, a wild Caucasian mountain tribe, for the performance of the Georgian *lezginka*, a dance which Petipa had mounted in the 1870s, based on movements shown him by four Circassian soldiers, and which Fokine now revised. Nijinsky's passionate virility was something no male dancer had exhibited on the Paris stage within memory. When the curtain fell another crowd surged backstage. Diaghilev pushed through it to embrace Karsavina and Nijinsky, and found a man mopping at Karsavina's bare arm, bleeding from a cut sustained on one of Nijinsky's jewels. Vaslav was dazedly trying to cope with question after question from the people surrounding him. They were asking, as people were always to ask, how he managed to pause in the air in the middle of a leap. Finally, he understood: 'Not difficult,' he said with characteristic naive humour; 'you just have to go up, and then pause a little, up there.'

What indeed was the nature of his leaps which

Le Festin was frankly a rather strange mélange: *music by several different composers, costumes by four different designers, performed in front of a backcloth painted for an opera. Dressed as a turbaned prince, Nijinsky danced Petipa's blue-bird* pas de deux *from the last act of* The Sleeping Beauty *with Karsavina as the bird, and later joined in a* pas classique *from* Raymonda; *as Karsavina said, it was 'happy confusion' – but brought the house down.*

Though other ballets were well received, it was Nijinsky's virile, flamboyant dancing in Fokine's divertissement, Le Festin, *that caused a sensation during the opening night of the Ballets Russes' Paris season on 18 May 1909. Next day, he woke to find himself famous – 'a prodigy', 'god of the dance'!*

so caught the imagination? Long after he had stopped dancing, those who had never seen him were to ask those fortunate enough to have been among Nijinsky's audiences about his famous jumps. The impression they made was supported by the performances of the other men in the company, for as Karsavina pointed out, great elevation was a speciality of the Russian school, and was to remain so. After the Second World War, something of the same effect was made by members of the Bolshoi and Kirov companies when they danced for the first time in London. Similarly, few people who were present when Rudolf Nureyev was first seen in England in 1961 will forget the impression of his leap onto the stage for his solo in the Black Swan *pas de deux* from *Swan Lake* – or the audience's reaction to it. More recently, even boys straight from the Royal Ballet School could, according to Karsavina, jump as high as Nijinsky – as with athletes, evolution raises all standards.

But in 1909 it seems to have been Nijinsky alone who could mesmerize his audiences into believing that he was able to defy gravity. There is, of course, a technical explanation. In a *grand jeté*, for instance, he would leap forward and upward, and then at the apogee of his jump subtly alter the balance of the back leg and the upper part of his body, drawing attention not so much to the progress of the jump as to the placing of the body, arms and head. In that split second he would, as Marie Rambert put it, 'consciously become himself, drawing our attention to that moment, so that we had the feeling that we saw him in the air as we had seen nobody else.' It is a technique which most good dancers have now mastered; but in 1909, it seemed like magic.

One should not under-estimate Karsavina's contribution to the partnership, nor the rapport between them – which included a sexual element, for Nijinsky at least. 'She excited me a little,' he wrote,

A major talent of Nijinsky's was his capacity to capture the very different character of different roles: his outgoing, high-spirited appearance in Le Festin *was remarkably different from his impersonation of a cowed puppet in* Petrushka *or the fey spirit of a flower in* Spectre de la Rose.

'because she was beautifully made . . . I courted her in Paris; my courtship was such as to make her feel that she attracted me. She felt this, but did not respond because she was married. I felt I had made a mistake, and kissed her hand. She understood that I wanted nothing from her, and felt happy.'

For the first press notices, Diaghilev had to wait for two days: they appeared after the first night on 19 May. This went equally well, before an almost equally fashionable audience which was again reduced by the end of the evening to screams of admiration and applause, and for some time simply declined to leave the theatre.

At last, Vaslav went off to dine triumphantly with Diaghilev and some friends at the Restaurant de l'Opéra, where the evening seems to have ended in an alcoholic haze in which, dimly, someone remembered seeing Sergei Pavlovitch placing a banana in the *décolletage* of the young Misia Sert.

Next morning, the newspapers were full of words and pictures (Vaslav had by now for the first time experienced a 'photo-call' and the attentions of gossip-writers as well as critics).

The notices were as enthusiastic as anyone – even Diaghilev – could wish. Nijinsky was 'a God of the dance', a 'prodigy', a very Vestris re-born (and for Vestris, after all, the British House of Commons had suspended a sitting so that its members could see him dance at the Opera House). Henri Gaudier-Vilars (better-known as 'Monsieur Willi', the husband of Colette) wrote of Nijinsky as a 'wonder of wonders, breaker of the record in *entrechats*... Yesterday when he took off so slowly and elegantly, describing a trajectory of four and a half metres and landing noiselessly in the wings, an incredulous gasp burst from the ladies.'

The audiences did not need the panegyrics of the critics to encourage them. Even those who entered the Châtelet with the determination not to be affected by the extraordinary stories they had heard of the magnificence of the evening were seduced within a few moments of the curtain rising. The Countess Anna de Noailles said that 'it was as if the creation of the world had added something to its seventh day ... I understood that I was witnessing a miracle. I was seeing something that had never before existed.' And Boris Kochno, who in 1923 was to become Diaghilev's secretary, and had by no means an uncritical eye, wrote later of Nijinsky in *Les Sylphides*: 'One had the impression of an unreal, weightless being, a spirit ... Watching Nijinsky move, one could not believe he was subject to the law of gravity, nor think that his breathing had to be rigidly controlled, that his movements required great effort ... The first appearance of Nijinsky on the Paris stage lives in my memory as a visitation of absolute beauty.'

The company settled down to enjoy its success, and to enjoy Paris. Now, even the humbler members of the *corps* were recognized in the streets, and would hear the whisper, '*Ce sont les Ballets Russes*', as they passed the students sitting at the café tables of the Boulevard Saint-Michel. Nijinsky, after his private class in the morning, would rehearse and then take a late lunch before going with Diaghilev to the Louvre, or to drive in the Bois. Then he would have a massage and sleep before the evening performance. Afterwards he would kiss his mother goodnight (she was always at the theatre in the evenings) before leaving with Diaghilev, often to dine with the group of friends – including Benois, Bakst and Roerich – with whom he was already discussing future plans.

There was also time for social *réclame*: he, Karsavina and Ida Rubenstein were constantly in demand for social occasions. Proust was seen escorting Karsavina and La Rubenstein was taken up by Comte Robert de Montesquieu, the model for the sinister Essientes in Huysmans' *A Rebours*. Diaghilev saw to it that no one but himself escorted Nijinsky, who often accompanied him to the exclusively male gatherings of which (as Karsavina, with her keen eyes, noted) the impresario was becoming the centre.

Diaghilev was now exclusively devoted to Vaslav. One cannot be sure when he broke off his intimate relationship with his handsome young secretary Alexis Mavrine, but not long after the Paris opening Mavrine suddenly left the city with one of the company's dancers, Olga Pedorova (who, ironically, Diaghilev had once said was the only woman he could conceivably love!). One cannot believe that, by then, Diaghilev was much concerned except at the blow to his pride.

Increasingly, he took Vaslav about with him –

and it is important to realize that this had the most crucial effect on the young man's development as an artist. The company they kept – Proust, the young Cocteau and the composer Reynaldo Hahn were among their regular companions – was that of men deeply interested in the arts, and Nijinsky was perhaps for the first time fully conscious of the world of art beyond the ballet. Karsavina remembered, for instance, watching him devouring with his eyes some of Gauguin's Polynesian paintings at the house of Emmanual Bibesco: 'Look at that strength!' he said. It is not difficult to see the effect those paintings had on his conception of *L'Après-Midi d'un Faune*.

On 2 June the company's second programme of ballets opened, including *Les Sylphides*. Now, for Paris, the ballet took its final form, danced to new orchestrations by no less than five composers, including Liadov, Glazunov, Tcherepnine and Stravinsky, whom Diaghilev had met in St Petersburg early in the year after a concert at which two of his early works were performed.

Diaghilev must have been curious, perhaps even apprehensive, about the reception of *Sylphides* and of Nijinsky in the part of the Poet. Quite apart from having no showy, brilliant solos, Vaslav was decked out in a really quite dreadful, epicene costume by Benois: a shirt with full, white sleeves beneath a long velvet jacket, a loose collar and full white scarf (over which the tresses of a long, blonde wig fell), and white tights through which the enormous muscles of his broad thighs showed very clearly. The comparison with Little Lord Fauntleroy is almost irresistible, and even Benois, who had designed the costume, had serious misgivings about it. But Vaslav and the three ballerinas – Karsavina, Preobrajenskaya and Pavlova – created a magical impression of dreamy softness and mystery, a conscious recapitulation or shadow of the romantic ballets of the previous century.

Nijinsky's inhabitation of the dream-like atmosphere of the ballet was complete. Later, in London, the critic Cyril Beaumont spoke of the sheer loveliness of his movements, of gestures which were like caresses, of the supreme technical control with which, for instance, he came slowly to rest after a pirouette, 'like a spinning wheel which has exhausted its momentum'.

With his infallible instinct for programme-building, Diaghilev followed *Les Sylphides* with *Cléopâtre*, the highly erotic romp based on *Nuit d'Egypte*, performed by Pavlova, Karsavina, Fokine, Nijinsky, Fedorova and Ida Rubenstein – who was borne on stage enclosed in an ebony and gold casket on the shoulders of six strapping male dancers. Removed from the casket, she proved to be wrapped, mummy-like, in twelve veils which slaves unwound one at a time to reveal her dressed in a ravishing Bakst negligée and a turquoise wig (her body was covered with light turquoise make-up). The ballet, and Bakst's costumes and décor (enormous pink gods towered over an Egyptian temple, the Nile seen between pillars at the back of the stage) created a new fashion in oriental design.

The season swept to its triumphant close in a strange mixture of rearranged programmes: *Cléopâtre* was so popular that Diaghilev slipped it in at the end of the opera *Ivan the Terrible* (in which Chaliapin triumphed), and *Le Pavillon d'Armide* was played after Serov's opera *Judith*.

The season at the Châtelet had been completely sold out, and the general enthusiasm was unanimous: even the critics had only one reservation – the quality of the music; they disliked the pot-pourri of pieces which made up the score of *Cléopâtre*, and the arrangements of Chopin's pieces for *Sylphides*. There was a special final gala at the Opéra (to which Diaghilev was hoping to bring the ballet next year), and then Diaghilev and Nijinsky went on a brief

Tamara Karsavina was the greatest of Nijinsky's partners; she created for Diaghilev the principal roles in Les Sylphides *(the Waltz),* Carnaval, Petrushka, *and* Spectre de la Rose *(in which she appeared with Nijinsky) and went on to create other major roles in* Thamar, Firebird, Daphnis and Chloe *and* Coq d'Or. *Later she danced in England for the Ballet Rambert.*

excursion to London, where they sat through a music-hall bill at the Coliseum and decided that to appear there would be beneath the company's dignity (though Nijinsky conceived an enormous admiration for the comedian Little Tich, who he ever afterwards referred to as 'The Littler').

On the evening of the Opéra gala on 10 June Vaslav had a sore throat, and failed to appear at a fête thrown by the Parisian socialite Madame Maurice Ephrussy on the following evening, though he had been offered a fee of a thousand francs (he received only 2,500 francs for the whole Paris season, in contrast to the 55,000 paid to the already celebrated Chaliapin. The franc at that time stood at around 25 to the pound sterling). Diaghilev called in a doctor, who diagnosed typhoid fever (those were the days when it was highly advisable to heed advice not to drink the Paris tap-water; Vaslav had unfortunately rushed to a tap to quench a violent thirst after a performance).

Vaslav was in bed for a month, nursed by his mother; even Bronia was not allowed to visit him. When she finally saw him, she found him sitting up in bed, his head completely shaved. Diaghilev, superstitiously terrified of any illness, had visited him and exchanged greetings from behind a half-open door. When it became possible, he took a small furnished flat and moved into it with Vaslav; now, in place of the small diamond ring given to him by Lvov, the dancer was seen to be wearing a sapphire set in platinum from Cartier's – Diaghilev's first present to him. Liota and Bronia were given a thousand francs, and went happily off to Italy for a short holiday near Pisa, before returning to St Petersburg. Diaghilev and Bakst accompanied Vaslav to Carlsbad, where the dancer rested, took drives through the woods and in general recuperated from the strenuous season and his illness. Bakst then took him to Venice, where Diaghilev was to join them after revisiting Paris to further his plans for the 1910 season. Vaslav marvelled at the alpine scenery of the train journey, and was enraptured by his first sight of Diaghilev's favourite city rising from the waters of the lagoon.

With his usual passion for sharing art with his protegés Diaghilev took Nijinsky around the Venetian palaces and galleries; but there was also time for relaxation. From the Grand Hôtel des Bains de Mer, on the Lido, Vaslav would swim – he was wonderfully at home in the water – or lie on the beach; and it was there that Bakst made a large portrait sketch of him dressed in red bathing drawers, a handkerchief about his head, only the rather self-conscious gesture of the left arm suggesting the dancer rather than the casual sunbathing holiday-maker.

It was in Venice that he was introduced to Isadora Duncan: he later told Bronia that the American dancer had proposed marriage to him ('Think what beautiful children we shall have!'). He also asked Bronia to send him a copy of *The Thousand and One Nights*. She did so, and later heard that it was during the Venetian holiday that the idea for *Schéhérazade* had first been mentioned.

After a fortnight, Diaghilev, Bakst and Nijinsky returned to Paris and then to St Petersburg, where the Maryinsky season was due to start at the beginning of September – Vaslav had a fortnight in which to get back into training. In the meantime Diaghilev was embroiled in the complexities of organizing a 1910 opera and ballet season at the Paris Opéra. As usual, financial difficulties were considerable – and Astruc, his Parisian colleague, was engaged in Machiavellian plots among which was a successful attempt to alienate Diaghilev, finally, from the Russian court – probably because he had discovered Diaghilev's own attempts to negotiate directly with the Opéra management, cutting Astruc out, but also because the latter was planning a season of Italian

A sketch of Nijinsky, elegant in evening dress, made in about 1909 by Valentin Serov, perhaps the most distinguished Russian painter of the time, and a close friend and colleague of Diaghilev.

opera and a visit of the Metropolitan Opera company from New York, and was thus in direct opposition to the Russian impresario.

To cut a long story short, the final blow to Diaghilev's plans for another opera season was the decision of Chaliapin, for various reasons, not to appear in Paris in 1910. This, however, forced Astruc and Diaghilev into collaboration (for the Frenchman had been counting on the Russian bass to appear with the Metropolitan company). There might be no Russian opera in Paris in 1910, but there would certainly be a ballet season – and plans for the repertoire were well under way: a score, *Daphnis and Chloe*, had been commissioned from Ravel, and another, *Le Dieu Bleu* from Reynaldo Hahn (to a libretto by Jean Cocteau). And increasingly noticeable in the background was another composer whose name was to be linked to those of Diaghilev and Nijinsky: Igor Stravinsky.

Igor Stravinsky. Though Stravinsky had written some music before meeting Diaghilev, the impresario shaped his early career, commissioning such works as Firebird, Petrushka, Sacre du Printemps *and later* Le Rossignol, Les Noces *and* Apollon Musagete. *He regarded Nijinsky as a musical ignoramus, but later admitted the greatness of the dancer's choreography for* Sacre.

CHAPTER III

The Continuing Legend 1909–1911

The 1909 season at the Maryinsky was not entirely comfortable for those dancers who had just returned from Paris. They found the entire organisation of the theatre thrown into disarray by the reports of Diaghilev's success: the old guard, led by Nicholas Legat and Kchessinskaya, felt obscurely that some sort of betrayal had gone on, and were certainly upset by the St Petersburg press, which treated Nijinsky as a returning hero – and an attractive one. A reporter from the *St Petersburg Gazette* recorded:

dressed modestly, shy, with a very boyish appearance, Nijinsky did not look like the hero of the brilliant Russian season in Paris, which scored such a success in that contemporary Babylon. He speaks just like a child. He gets worked up and blushes just as if he is embarrassed by his celebrity.

But the Maryinsky management was increasingly tough on him. Colonel V.A. Teliakovsky, the Director of the Imperial Theatres, highly irritated at Diaghilev's success as an impresario, took his irritation out on Vaslav, who was regularly fined for being late at rehearsal, or some other minor infringement of company rules, and as a result himself became increasingly sullen and careless in his work.

On their side, the dancers who had taken part in the Paris season – The 'Diaghilevtsy', as they were known – felt that the Maryinsky directors were backward-looking and over-traditional, were highly critical of Legat's re-staging of Drigo's old ballet *Le Talisman* as dull and boring, and resented the hours of rehearsal Legat demanded.

When Nijinsky and Karsavina danced Giselle *in Paris in 1910, the old ballet had not been seen there for over forty years. Nijinsky worried more about this role than perhaps any other, concerned to re-create the 1841 ballet for his own time, and to play the Prince not as a mere dancing role, but as a real characterization.*

In the event, Nijinsky had a personal success in *Le Talisman* (the critics suggested that the enormous Maryinsky stage looked too small for this extraordinary dancer): and he was very excited by the prospect of dancing in *Giselle* with Pavlova, which was in rehearsal throughout the autumn of 1909. Bronia always insisted that the St Petersburg rehearsals of *Giselle* were the most perfect ballet performances she ever saw; the members of the *corps* were moved to tears by Vaslav's mime of grief in the second act, and his entire devotion to the interpretation of his role was unforgettable.

Pavlova, somehow, did not arouse quite the same enthusiasm, and eventually, to everyone's surprise, it was announced that the partnership was dissolved before it could be seen by the public. Both dancers would appear in *Giselle*, but not together. Bronia asked Pavlova the reason, and the latter quite frankly explained that she had no intention of being overshadowed by Nijinsky. He could fill the theatre on his own; she would be much happier if audiences who came to see her dance were not distracted by his performance.

Vaslav was not unduly concerned. By the time Pavlova gave her *Giselle* at the Maryinsky in January 1910, he was focusing on the coming Paris season, and spent every free evening at Diaghilev's flat with the small group of associates engaged in making final plans. One of them was Stravinsky.

Diaghilev had been introduced to Stravinsky in February 1909, after a concert at which his *Fantastic Scherzo* and *Feu d'Artifice* had been performed. They quickly became friends, and Diaghilev commissioned him – he was then twenty-seven – to orchestrate Chopin's *Valse Brillante* for the finale of *Les Sylphides*. A year later the composer was one of the group of friends who regularly took tea at Diaghilev's flat to discuss plans for the 1910 season.

In 1909, Nikolai Legat re-staged Le Talisman, *an old ballet sometimes known as* La Fille en l'Air, *and Nijinsky danced the part of Zephyr with such magnificence that it was renamed the Hurricane; he jumped so high that his head disappeared above the hangings of the Imperial Theatre stage.*

It seemed important to produce at least one purely Russian work for that season. Fokine began looking through Russian fairy stories; Walter Nouvel, a childhood friend of Diaghilev, pressed the claims of a story by a young poet, Prince Gregori Alexandrovich Potemkin, with whom he was in love, and Alexy Mikhailovich Remizov, an eccentric surrealist writer, contributed many original ideas which quickly crystallized into the plot of *The Firebird* (the scenario of which was eventually credited solely to Fokine).

At first it was taken for granted that Tcherepnine was to write the score; then, independently, Diaghilev approached Liadov and commissioned him. But when a mutual friend met him some weeks later and enquired how the score was going on, Liadov replied: 'Fine. I've bought the music paper.'

Nijinksy as Albrecht in Giselle *is shown by the photographer Bert wearing trunks over his tights, in a style adopted by male dancers at the Maryinsky; it was his exchanging these for Benois' costume, which seemed offensive to Russian eyes, that brought about his dismissal from the theatre.*

Diaghilev panicked at this, and mentioned the matter to Stravinsky, who not only knew about the ballet but confessed that he had already sketched out some ideas for a score. He promised to finish the work by March, and have it orchestrated within another fortnight.

The Firebird was intended for Pavlova. But what of Nijinsky? Despite Diaghilev's doubt as to whether a Parisian audience would be interested in a Russian interpretation of a French work, the first role suggested for him in the coming season was apparently that of Albrecht in *Giselle*. Diaghilev had at first hoped that Pavlova would dance the title role; others wondered whether this was likely – and indeed she now announced that she had signed a contract to appear at the Palace Theatre, London, as part of a music-hall bill, and would not be available for Paris. Already Karsavina had signed with the London Coliseum; she too would be unavailable. Things were beginning to look very grim. Diaghilev began feverishly courting Karsavina, hoping to persuade her to wriggle out of her London contract and replace Pavlova in *Giselle*. He was also busily trying to persuade Rimsky-Korsakov's widow to allow him to mount the symphonic poem *Schéhérazade* as a ballet – a scheme on which Benois, in particular, was very keen, intending to write the libretto while Bakst (who had put the idea to Diaghilev in Venice) prepared designs. But the task was a difficult one, for just before his death the composer had expressed his horror at the idea that Isadora Duncan should lay hands on the score. Meanwhile, Stravinsky had been commissioned to prepare, from pieces by other composers, a score for a short *divertissement* to be called *Les Orientales*.

Now came a stroke of fate which would add to the repertory of Diaghilev's company one of its most successful ballets. In March, the proprietors of *Satyricon*, an arts magazine, gave a ball at the

Pavlova Hall in Troitsky Street, and Fokine was asked to stage a ballet. He had for some time wanted to choreograph a ballet based on the traditional characters of the *commedia dell'arte* – Pierrot, Pantalon, Columbine and Harlequin. He began to mount one using some Clementi sonatas, but for the ball turned to Schumann's piano suite 'Scenes Mignonnes', and devised a suite of dances which he called *Carnaval*.

As soon as they heard the news, members of the Maryinsky company were anxious to be asked to appear in the new ballet – despite the fact that the administration jealously issued a notice reminding them that to appear anywhere but in their own theatre would break their contracts of employment. The dancers ignored the hint – except that they appeared masked. They may have been slightly worried when they recognized several members of the administration in the audience at the ball; but the officials pretended not to recognize anyone, and not a single fine was imposed.

Nijinsky (at that time appearing twice a week in the usual Maryinsky repertory) appeared as Florestan, Karsavina as Columbine, Bronia as Papillon, Leonide Leontiev as Harlequin, Vera Fokina as Chiarina. Though Fokine outlined it, it was Vaslav who invented the movements of his sister's 'Butterfly Dance' – probably his first piece of public choreography.

Sergei Grigoriev, Diaghilev's *répétiteur*, was at the ball and described *Carnaval* to him; Benois, too, had been delighted by it – and fortunately orchestrations of the original piano score already existed, though by a number of composers – Rimsky-Korsakov, Glazunov, Liadov and Tcherepnine. Diaghilev agreed to include a fully worked version of the piece in the Paris season.

By that financial alchemy of which he was always to be capable, Diaghilev had succeeded in introducing enough guarantees to make a season at the Opéra possible. He had succeeded in persuading Karsavina to try to get out of her Coliseum season – or rather to get leave of absence by promising to return to London the moment the Paris season was over. She may have been encouraged by increasing rapport with Vaslav, who now called her 'Tatotchka' and obviously enjoyed working with her.

Rehearsals started in April, with a great deal of work being done on *L'Oiseau de Feu*, Stravinsky supervising the playing of his score – and sometimes joining the rehearsal pianist on the single piano in the pit of the Distorting Mirror Theatre. The company at first found the new and original score very difficult – Fokine's choreography was also original and sometimes difficult to grasp, but gradually the dancers came to terms with it. Then Fokine turned his attention to *Schéhérazade*, in which Nijinsky was to dance the role of a Negro slave. He was not at first seen at general rehearsals, but worked privately with Fokine and Ida Rubenstein, who was playing the Princess Zobeide.

The enthusiasm of the company was enormous: rehearsals went on late into the night, and even after they had finished work the dancers would sit around with the scene-painters and musicians, often joined by Diaghilev, discussing the new ballets. Diaghilev always knew how to inspire enthusiasm and loyalty, and the least significant member of his company felt an important, even vital, part of the team.

On the way to Paris, there were performances at the Theater des Westens in a suburb of Berlin. *Carnaval* went extremely well there, and *Cléopâtre* so impressed the German Emperor that he ordered the members of a congress of archaeologists, meeting in the city, to attend a performance – presumably because he thought it would be well for them to see what life in ancient Egypt had really been like.

Rehearsals for *Schéhérazade* at the Paris

Opéra were rather worrying: a number of extras had been engaged to fill out the final scene; Fokine, who could not speak French, found it difficult to control them, and kept losing his temper, which in any event was not especially serene; he always had a keen sense of his own importance, and was dissatisfied with the amount of advance publicity afforded him in the French press, compared with that which was focused on Nijinsky, the 'god of the dance.'

The opening might have been something of an anti-climax after the furore of 1909: after all, neither Pavlova nor Karsavina were able to appear, and it was in any case a distinct risk to have planned a season consisting entirely of ballet – no opera, no Chaliapin to help raise the temperature. Nevertheless, all the tickets for the season were sold, and the opening night (4 June) dispelled any doubts that might have lingered.

The evening began with a mixture of *divertissements* from *Le Festin* and *Prince Igor*. Then came *Carnaval*, with Nijinsky as Papillon; and finally, *Schéhérazade*. And it was *Schéhérazade* that, this season, was to have the greatest effect.

Diaghilev had finally succeeded in persuading Rimsky-Korsakov's widow to allow him to use the music. The composer had always denied that the score had any coherent 'programme', though it had been inspired by images drawn from the Arabian Nights Tales. Benois and Fokine had constructed a narrative concerning the unfaithfulness of the wives of Shah Shahrir, King of India. While Shahrir is hunting, there is an eleborate orgy (to the music Rimsky-Korsakov headed 'Festival at Bagdad: the Sea'); he returns to slaughter his wives' lovers, and in particular the Golden Slave, the lover of his favourite wife Zobeida, who then kills herself in her grief. The curtain falls on the grieving Shah.

The Paris audience was immediately captivated by Bakst's setting. The curtain rose on a vast hall,

Photographs of Nijinsky as the Golden Slave in Fokine's Schéhérazade *(1910) seem now somewhat 'camp'; but the evidence is that the passion and grace of his performance stunned his audiences.*

which in fact consisted of great folds of curtaining falling to a carpeted floor on which piles of bright-coloured loose cushions were piled. It was the riot of colour that astonished the onlookers. Colours which no one but Bakst would have thought of placing together had an almost physical effect: tomato red, malachite, rose-pink, lapis. Against this background, lit by huge lamps, the colours of the costumes moved and glowed: the blues and crimsons of the robes of the kings of India and Persia, the green and pink of

For Nijinsky as the Golden Slave in Schéhérazade *Bakst created a costume of cloth of gold, with loose trousers of gold brocade, and gave him a silvery-grey make-up which made him look like a living statue. The scene in which Ida Rubenstein danced while he wound his body around her, but without ever touching her, was astonishingly erotic.*

the dresses of the Odalisques, a Chief Eunuch in violent scarlet, Negro slaves in jewelled brassières and metallic lamé trousers and Janissaries in orange-vermillion and chrome-yellow. Proust, writing to Reynaldo Hahn, said: 'I never saw anything so beautiful.'

The designs were to influence Parisian and later London fashion in a variety of ways. Richard Buckle says that Cartier set sapphires and emeralds together for the first time in the West after seeing *Schéhérazade.* The *couturiers* were influenced both by designs and fabrics, producing dresses in heavy silk brocades and *brocatelles* flecked with gold, silver and steel, or embroidered with fantastic designs in the vivid colours of Bakst's staging. Paul Poiret, the designer (whose house took up orientalism with particular enthusiasm) threw a magnificent summer party in 1911 on the theme of *The 1002nd Night*, at which three hundred guests were dressed as ancient Persians, with Poiret himself as Sultan in a white jewelled turban and a pale grey quilted kaftan edged with fur and belted in green silk. A gold cage full of exotic slaves stood in the grounds of his Paris house, and white peacocks and flamingoes ranged with parrots, macaws and monkeys chained to the trees above them. Indoors, the guests reclined on huge cushions like those of Bakst's set, to watch *divertissements* which included a dance by a nude white slave-girl swathed in a cloud of gauze. The party was to publicize Poiret's Oriental Collection, which included harem pantaloons and 'lampshade' tunics, and was almost entirely inspired by *Schéhérazade* (though Poiret tried to deny it).

The ballet's influence continued for years, and in many parts of the world. In Paris, women who might have walked out of a seraglio attended the Opéra; a year later, Lady Cunard appeared at Covent Garden in a Russian diadem; later still, when the Diaghilev Ballet was appearing in Boston, the

Evening Transcript reported that 'in the shops meek-faced housewives in sober and godly raiment are trying on scarves *à la Bakst, chapeaux* Reveller, evening gowns *couleur de faune....*'

But quite apart from the spectacle of *Schéhérazade*, there was of course the dancing. Here, too, the ballet proved a winner. The *corps* was impressive enough; and Ida Rubenstein as Zobeida – 'excessively beautiful, like a liqueur from poison fragrances,' said Cocteau. But attention was concentrated on Nijinsky as the Golden Slave. Fokine, whose opinion of Vaslav as a man was scarcely higher than his opinion of him as a choreographer, was as always generous in praise of his dancing. The 'lack of masculinity' which he believed made Nijinsky unfit for certain roles made him ideal as the Slave: he seemed half-animal, half-man – half-masculine, half-feminine, 'softly leaping great distances, now a stallion with distended nostrils, full of energy, overflowing with an abundance of power, his feet impatiently pawing the ground.'

He leaped from the golden door from which a eunuch released him, dressed in trousers of gold brocade, gold bracelets and jewels sparkling against the blue-grey make-up which covered his body, and with an enormously wild jump which seemed to cover the whole vast stage hurled himself onto the divan on which Zobeida lay, winding his body around hers. Cocteau described him as jumping 'like a young beast of prey that has been kept locked up in darkness and is now intoxicated by the light. His movements are sudden, like a tiger's; he reels with happiness; he gives out mute cries; his dark face is illumined by his white teeth; sensuously, he stretches out on the pillows where his gold body undulates, like a fish gleaming in the sun.'

The most vivid description was written by the British ballet critic Cyril Beaumont, in his *The Diaghilev Ballet in London* (1940):

Fokine himself thought Nijinsky in the role of the Golden Slave was like a primitive savage: half-human, half-feline, like a powerful stallion in his vigour and power.

Nijinsky as the Negro wore a gold handkerchief tied on his head; baggy gold trousers, tight at the waist and ankles, but of a shimmering fullness elsewhere; and a gold band over his chest. He was made up not black, but a curious shade of dark blue, not unlike the bloom on black grapes ... When the Chief Eunuch (Enrico Cecchetti) in obedience to Zobeida's menacing threat (a lascivious Ida Rubenstein) had reluctantly opened the last door, Nijinsky shot out of his room like an arrow from a bow in a mighty parabola which enabled him to cross in one bound a good two-thirds of the width of the stage ... the actual effect was as though he leaped from a crouching position, the kind of leap a tiger might make.

There was another great moment for him at the end of the ballet, when Shahrir, who had only feigned to depart on a hunting-expedition, suddenly returned and was confronted by the scene of orgy. In a merciless rage, he ordered slaves and women to be put to the sword. The Gold Negro was the last of the victims, and it was a thrilling experience to see him now darting this way and that, now doubling on his pursuers in a desperate, frenzied anxiety to escape the avenging scimitars. But a blade flashed and he fell headlong, to spin on the back of his neck with his legs thrust rigid in the air. The simulated death scene invariably aroused a storm of well-merited applause, for, apart from the rare skill obviously essential to its performance, it looked dangerous in the extreme.

There is little doubt that, as it was first seen, *Schéhérazade* resembled nothing so much as a visualization of the popular soft pornography of the time (the novels of Pierre Loti or Joris-Karl Huysmans, for instance), made acceptable by the genius of the designer, choreographer and performers. By the time the work ended, even those who might have had reservations about the subject-matter or its treatment were entirely captivated and amazed by the ballet's final moments. Francis de Miomandre described them:

When the executioner's sword pierced him in the final tumult we no longer really knew whether he had succumbed to the avenging steel or to the unbearable violence of his joy in those three fierce somersaults.

Estrade Guerra remembered how Nijinsky 'fell forwards, pivoted on his head, then fell back on the other side, his arms and legs completely slack... It was like seeing a hare wounded by the huntsman's shot and rising before the final fall.'

Karsavina, having persuaded Sir Oswald Stoll to release her for the Paris season, arrived not long after the first night, and rehearsals of *Giselle* began. These were difficult. Because of his intense preoccupation with the character and the plot, Nijinsky at first seemed very ill-at-ease at rehearsals with Karsavina, lacked conviction in the conventional mime demanded by the ballet, and desperately wanted to make Albrecht's dilemma real and moving to a contemporary audience. Karsavina, many years later, comparing Nijinsky's accomplishments with those of a popular new star, Nureyev (who had just danced a spectacular Albrecht opposite the Giselle of Margot Fonteyn), was to say that the only thing in which Nijinsky was truly incomparable in the part was mime. At rehearsal, she found this difficult to take; other Albrechts were preoccupied with dancing – Nijinsky with building the character. The Russian critic Vera Krasovskaya goes so far as to suggest that *Giselle* was 'the only ballet in which Nijinsky was able to free himself from his mask and express his individuality to the full in the pure form of the classical dance.'

But whatever the cause of the difficulty, difficulty there was. Nijinsky grew sullen. Karsavina was reduced to tears. Diaghilev did his best to mediate between them.

The public did not take to *Giselle* (which had not been seen in Paris since 1868) as to the purely Russian works in the company's repertory. Proust's friend the composer Reynaldo Hahn thought it 'celebrated but insipid', yet Karsavina was much

Watching her brother rehearse Giselle *with Anna Pavlova was something Bronia Nijinska never forgot: over seventy years later she wrote of the 'great gift to us artists' of being able to see 'those two geniuses of the dance' as Albrecht and Giselle. But it was Karsavina who danced the title-role in public.*

applauded in it, and so was Nijinsky. While Kochno found his acting lacking in expression (when Giselle was going mad, Vaslav stood aside, motionless, 'acting with his eyes' as he told Diaghilev), Benois said that he 'made the grief of the repentant seducer profoundly pathetic'. By general consent his performance in the last act, when the Wilis attempt to make Albrecht dance himself to death, was magnificent – 'genuinely terrifying', Benois remarked – and the existing photographs (by Bert) of Nijinsky in the part are noble and impressive. Later, it is worth recording, Karsavina said that after all she much enjoyed dancing with Nijinsky in the ballet: 'In one respect he was unique – in the way that one could feel at one with him. For classical *pas de deux*, of course, I would have preferred a taller partner, because he could lift me higher. But Vaslav was quite strong at lifts, and he was a very inspiring partner. We simply loved dancing with each other.'

Learning Giselle *with Nijinsky 'was not without tears, and many', wrote Karsavina; reconciling her classical conception of the ballet to Nijinsky's desire to re-make it in terms of the twentieth century was difficult. The public regarded the ballet as oldfashioned fustian; but the photographs suggest that we would now find these performances enthralling.*

Someone who was impressed by the revival was Colonel Teliakovsky, who had come to Paris to see Diaghilev's season, and after the first performance of *Giselle* came backstage to assure Nijinsky that the ballet would definitely be presented at the Maryinsky in the autumn with himself and Pavlova in the leading roles.

Apart from *Giselle*, Karsavina's arrival in Paris meant that rehearsals of *L'Oiseau de Feu*, or *Firebird*, could start. After Pavlova's refusal of the title role (the suggestion that she declined it because she hated Stravinsky's music seems unfounded), Nijinsky had tried to persuade Diaghilev to allow him to dance it: after all, he had had a success as the Bluebird, and moreover was perfectly capable of dancing on his points (something not normally done by male dancers). It would have been a fascinating experiment, but probably wisely, Diaghilev was adamant that it should be a female role, and Nijinsky played no part in the tremendous success of the ballet. He did, however, appear with Karsavina, Ekaterina Geltzer and Alexandre Volinine, Alexandra Vassilieva and Georgi Rosai in *Les Orientales*, dancing two solo numbers – *Kobold*, in which he was a goblin capering to a piece by Grieg (orchestrated by Stravinsky), and *Danse Siamoise*, to music by Christian Sinding, which consisted mainly of rather static poses based on dances which Fokine had seen performed by a group of Siamese dancers in St Petersburg some years previously. The dances had been choreographed, originally, for a performance at the Maryinsky in February – on the same evening on which *Carnaval* was first performed, and interestingly the *St Petersburg Gazette* had remarked on that occasion that the dances would be the first to be performed by a *premier danseur classique* as a soloist, and not merely a partner or *porteur*. The splendid, bejewelled Siamese costume he wore for the last dance is familiar through a series of photographs taken of Vaslav by Jacques-Emile Blanche in a garden at Passy, while Cocteau stood nearby and sketched him.

Danse Siamoise *was one of two* divertissements *performed under the title* Les Orientales: *it seems to have been more a collection of poses than a conventional piece of choreography.*

In 1910, Nijinsky was photographed in a garden at Passy for the painter Jacques-Emiles Blanche, who wanted to paint his portrait in the costume he wore for a solo Fokine had contrived for him, based on the movements of a group of Siamese dancers he had seen in St Petersburg. The dance has not survived, but there are perhaps more photographs and drawings of Nijinsky in this costume than in any other.

The season was so successful that extra performances were given at the Opéra – before which there was a flying visit to Brussels for two performances at the Theatre de la Monnaie during the International Exposition. Adolf Bolm, the enormously popular and powerful dancer who had created the role of the Tartar Chief in the Polovtsian Dances from *Prince Igor* was not available, and Nijinsky volunteered to learn the role; for once he was less than successful, admitting that for physical as well as temperamental reasons he was unable to equal Bolm's display of sheer force and savagery.

Plans for a visit to London after the close of the Paris season had been cancelled because of the death of King Edward VII; the space was filled by extra

Right and below
Photographs of Nijinsky in the Danse Siamoise, *though the dance was a very minor one, were released to the British Press to publicize his visits to England – partly because the East was much in fashion in 1911.*

Paris performances, when Nijinsky danced Harlequin in *Carnaval* – a performance which captivated audiences by his gaiety and lightness; it must indeed have been one of his most enchanting roles, as the photographs show, his costume (including white tights with lozenges of colour painted directly onto them, and a black mask painted on his face in greasepaint) contributing to the effect. The final movement of his variation, when he pirouetted so fast that he seemed a blur, imperceptibly sinking until he ended up sitting on the stage facing the audience, always brought a storm of applause.

During the 1910 season Diaghilev once more took pains to involve Vaslav with the most intelligent of his friends; by the time the impresario and the dancer went off once more to Venice (after two performances in Brussels), Nijinsky seems to have been giving some thought to the possibility of choreographing a ballet – no doubt encouraged by Diaghilev, who felt bound to contrive a success for him in 1911 which would equal that achieved by Fokine with his latest ballet, *The Firebird*.

Stravinsky was supposed to be at work on the score which would eventually become *Le Sacre du Printemps* or *The Rite of Spring*, and in September, Diaghilev and Nijinsky travelled from Venice to meet the composer at Lausanne to discover how the score progressed. There, Stravinsky surprised them with an altogether new and unexpected work: it had started out as a piano concerto, but now, combined with another work, it was to become the score of *Petrushka*. Petrushka is the Russian equivalent of Mr Punch (though a much more sympathetic figure), and it appears that listening to Stravinsky's purely orchestral work, Diaghilev heard a sound which he thought might be the cry of such a puppet. On the other hand, Stravinsky later claimed that he had already entitled the piece 'Petrushka's Cry'. But whoever originated the idea, it was decided that it fitted the score like a glove, and that Benois should be asked to write a libretto and to design the ballet. Though there had recently been a gigantic row between Benois and Diaghilev (stemming from the fact that, most unjustly, Benois' name had been omitted from the programme of *The Firebird*, in which Bakst was credited with the libretto), he agreed.

Back in St Petersburg, a notice appeared on the Maryinsky noticeboard calling rehearsals on 20 August for *Giselle*, which was to open the 1910 autumn season on 4 September: 'Giselle – Mme Pavlova; Albrecht – M. Nijinsky.' But the partnership seemed doomed, for a letter came from Venice with a doctor's certificate disclosing that Vaslav had severe sunstroke. The management, obviously suspecting chicanery, replied that he must return immediately or his salary would cease. But he did not appear, and the opening performance was cancelled. Pavlova, in transit between London and America, had been free only for that evening; *Giselle* was re-scheduled for 26 September, with Karsavina and Nijinsky. Still he did not appear, though there was news that he had been seen in Paris with Diaghilev, apparently completely recovered.

He had in fact been terrified to receive, while genuinely ill with sunstroke in Venice, notification that he should report for military service. Doctors' certificates, and a letter requesting exemption on the grounds that he was the sole supporter of his mother, had only succeeded in deferring his call-up until September 1911.

At the end of November, 1910, he at last re-appeared in St Petersburg. Presumably only his increasing fame saved him from severe punishment. As it was, Teliakovsky did not even attempt a reprimand; a performance of *Giselle* with Karsavina was announced for January.

The rivalry between the traditionalists and the Diaghilevtsy-Fokinsky faction was renewed. The veteran Kchessinskaya now led the traditionalist faction. Nijinsky had infuriated her by declining an invitation to partner her at a benefit celebrating her twenty years at the Imperial Theatre, and she vowed not to rest until he was dismissed together with his sister and everyone around him.

Fortunately for the Diaghilevtsys, Teliakowsky tended to side with them. He and Kchessinskaya had never got on, he was discontented with the theatre's repertory, and had been excited by what he had seen in Paris.

Nijinsky was beginning to be preoccupied with his constantly developing ideas of a new kind of choreography – he had perhaps already begun to work out ideas for *L'Après-Midi d'un Faune*.

Diaghilev, meanwhile, was doing more than planning a programme for another Paris season – he was planning his own permanent ballet company, whose performances would not have to be confined simply to the periods when dancers were not needed in St Petersburg. Karsavina was by now a prima ballerina at the Maryinsky, which gave her the right to dance abroad as a guest artiste. Adolf Bolm, who had appeared in the first Paris season and had been second only to Nijinsky in arousing the admiration of the audience, had served the five years required of graduates from the School, and was free to resign and join Diaghilev on a permanent basis. But Nijinsky?

The difficulty was that he had only left the School in 1907, and unless he broke his agreement with the theatre would have to remain a member of its company until 1912. To break the contract was unthinkable; there seemed no way out of the difficulty – and for Diaghilev a company not led by Vaslav was equally unthinkable.

On Sunday, 5 February 1911, Nijinsky was scheduled to partner Karsavina in *Giselle* – the first time he had danced Albrecht in St Petersburg. The events of that evening have been rehearsed many times, and none of the accounts of it are thoroughly reliable. But it seems that Vaslav decided to wear, in the first act, (when Albrecht is disguised as a peasant) the costume designed for the Paris production by Benois. Benois' designs were reminiscent of the earlier productions of the ballet when Perrot had danced it in the 1840s – a green and red tunic ending in a short skirt falling over the thighs. Diaghilev, it is said, thought this skirt too long, and ordered it to be shortened so that the line of the leg could be properly seen.

For the events which followed, it may be best to accept the memory of Vaslav's sister Bronia. In her autobiography (in which her memory for dates and people sometimes lets her down, but which in general seems accurate – and after all, she was there at the time) she says that the evening went well. In the audience was the Dowager Empress Maria Fedorovna, several Grand Dukes, and many courtiers. They all seem to have thoroughly approved of the performance, and there was continuous enthusiastic applause.

Next morning, however, Nijinsky was awakened by the telephone, and asked to come to the office of Alexander Dmitrievitch Krupensky, the Administrator to the Directorate of the St Petersburg Imperial Theatres. Vaslav, Bronia and Liota took it for granted that he was to be congratulated on his success, and perhaps offered the position of *premier danseur* (he was still technically only a *coryphé*).

When he returned home, however, he announced that His Highness Count Fredericks, Minister of the Imperial Court and responsible directly to the Tsar for the affairs of the Imperial Theatres, had telephoned Krupensky to insist that Nijinsky should be immediately dismissed for offending the Dowager Empress by appearing before her 'in an indecent and improper costume'. Krupensky had no option but to obey, though he suggested that if Vaslav sent an immediate apology to Fredericks he would no doubt be reinstated in due course.

Nijinsky on the contrary suggested that it was the Imperial Theatre that should apologize to him, and left. He telephoned Diaghilev to announce that he was now available to become a full-time artist of the Ballets Russes.

There are still, of course, mysterious aspects to the affair. Karsavina, for instance, always said that the Empress summoned her to the royal box during the interval to compliment her on her London success, and made no reference to her partner, while Count Beckendorff, Grand Marshal of the Imperial Court, later told Vaslav that the Empress was astonished to hear that she was supposed to have been shocked: 'I did not see anything indecent in Nijinsky's costume,' she had told him, 'on the contrary, I was full of admiration for him. If I had noticed anything shocking, then as a lady I would hardly have drawn attention to it.' The photographs of Nijinsky as Albrecht could not remotely be considered offensive, and the greatest possible allowances for changing standards of taste or decency still fail to persuade one that any serious complaint can have been made. On the other hand one newspaper, a vulgar sheet called the *St Petersburg Feuilleton*, did draw attention to the costume: 'What was really smart was in the "inexpressibles",' its gossip-writer said, in a Dickensian phrase; so the costume must have struck some people as unusual.

Discussion has been endless, but the solution in fact seems a relatively simple one. Count Beckendorff told Vaslav, later, that the Dowager Empress had said, 'It must all have been a joke by the boys. . . .' 'The boys' were the two Grand Dukes, Sergei Mikhailovitch and Andrei Vladimirovitch. The latter had indeed come backstage during the interval and asked to examine Vaslav's costume, which he had found 'indecent'. Vaslav had sent a message from his dressing-room that he was not dressed, and was making-up for Act II, but eventually came down and briefly revealed his costume to the Duke, who seemed satisfied. But it was Vladimirovitch who had later reported the Dowager Empress' alleged embarrassment; and it is worth recalling that his mistress for the past ten years had been none other than Kchessinskaya, who had sworn to engineer Vaslav's dismissal from the company. It is difficult not to draw certain conclusions.

At all events, to his mother's despair, Vaslav was no longer a member of the company, and though Teliakovsky (who had been away from St Petersburg when the incident occurred) appealed to him to return, he resolutely declined. Bronia now decided to resign from the company, too. Adolf Bolm followed their example. One can understand why. Yes, they would lose the guaranteed pension which would have been theirs on retirement from the Maryinsky, but they had tasted a kind of fame, a quality of *réclame* in Paris which Russia could not offer. Even today, Russian audiences are notably less demonstrative than their Western counterparts; once tasted, as other Russian dancers have demonstrated, adulation of the kind shown by Western audiences is seductive. And life in the West was attractive, too – particularly, perhaps, life in Paris. Karsavina has written of the enchantment she felt on first visiting that city; Grigoriev had been entranced by it; Lydia Lopokova actually fainted with pleasure when she first experienced it.

Finally, but perhaps most importantly, the repertory at the Maryinsky was dull and unimaginative, and the more talented young dancers and choreographers were champing at the bit. It seemed that, as a French newspaper of the time put it, 'Everything that is talented is trampled underfoot in Russia.' Diaghilev offered more exciting fare – the chance for young artists to enlarge themselves, make new ballets, tackle new and exciting roles, reach out into the twentieth century. The situation at the Maryinsky was to remain the same well into the 1960s and 1970s, when several members of the Kirov company (the Maryinsky was re-named after the revolution) and its rival, the Bolshoi, defected to the West for precisely the same reasons that had weighed so heavily with their predecessors fifty years previously.

Diaghilev, busily signing contracts for his own company, set out to wring the utmost publicity from the incident, cabling Astruc with the bare details: 'VESTRIS DISMISSED REASON COSTUME DESIGNED BAKST STOP MONSTROUS

INTRIGUE STOP APPALLING SCANDAL STOP USE PUBLICITY.' Four days later: 'INCRIMINATING COSTUME SAME AS PARIS STOP GISELLE STYLE CARPACCIO STOP WORRIED DIRECTION INVENT DOWAGER DEMANDED DISMISSAL STOP LETS STIR SOMETHING UP.' An hour later: 'WHOLE FAMILY PRESENT APPLAUDED STOP MOTHER SEEING FOR FIRST TIME DECLARED SHE HAD NEVER SEEN ANYTHING LIKE IT STOP NEXT DAY DIRECTION GAVE OUT MOTHER SHOCKED INSISTED DISMISSAL.'

The Diaghilev Ballet Company was to appear in Monte Carlo in the winter, and in Rome. There would be the Paris season in June, followed hopefully by the Coronation season in London, and perhaps an American tour. The repertory would consist of *The Firebird, Schéhérazade, Narcisse, Petrushka, Sadko, Le Dieu Bleu, Le Spectre de la Rose* and a ballet to music by Liszt (which in fact never materialised). In mid-March Bakst arrived in Paris to prepare the sets, and on 18 March Diaghilev and Nijinsky took the train from St Petersburg for the three-day journey to France. Nijinsky, though he

Asked to produce a poster for the 1913 season of the Ballets Russes, Jean Cocteau drew Nijinsky in a pose from the Danse Siamoise, *but dressed him in a notional costume for* Le Spectre de la Rose *(without ever having seen the ballet). The result was one of two famous posters advertising the Ballets.*

The Monte Carlo Opera House, c., 1912, when the Ballets Russes gave a season there.

could not have suspected it, was in fact leaving Russia for the last time.

After a brief weekend in Paris, they went on to Nice and Monte Carlo; gradually, in ones and twos, members of the company began to assemble, and to take class under Cecchetti. Members of the *corps* came from St Petersburg, Moscow, Poland, Paris. The Maryinsky had rather generously given several girls a year's leave of absence in order to join the company. Fokine was given the title of Choreographic Director, Benois that of Artistic Director (with overall charge of productions), and the *régisseur* was Sergei Leonidovitch Grigoriev.

The new ballets slowly began to come together, and the season opened on 9 April with Nijinsky and

In 1911, Karsavina played Zobeida, unfaithful wife of the King of India, in Schéhérazade *(a part created for Ida Rubenstein); here she is seen with Nijinsky as her lover, the Golden Slave.*

The interior of the Monte Carlo Opera House.

Karsavina in *Giselle* and *Schéhérazade* – on the same night, displaying a remarkable range.

It was on 19 April that the first new ballet of the Monte Carlo season, *Le Spectre de la Rose*, was played. Nominally, it was a ballet for two characters, though virtually a male solo. Fokine had had the idea, it is said, while watching the scene in *Carnaval* in which Chiarina threw a rose to Eusebius. Later, a critic writing about that ballet had placed at the head of his article two lines from Gautier's poem *Le Spectre de la Rose*:

> *Je suis le spectre d'une rose*
> *Que tu portais hier au bal.*

and later wrote to Bakst suggesting that a short ballet could be made on the idea of a girl returning from a ball and dreaming that the spirit of a rose she had carried came to dance with her. He also suggested Weber's 'Invitation to the Dance' as a possible score. The ballet had been created by Fokine in a few days, in St Petersburg.

This, the most famous of all Karsavina/Nijinsky ballets, has been danced many times by other artists – but more often than not has appeared effete and silly. It is one of those pieces forever attached to the characters of two particular performers (perhaps the best-known modern example is Ashton's *Marguerite and Armand*, created for Fonteyn and Nureyev). When Bronia saw it first, in rehearsal in St Petersburg, she found the choreography disappointingly conventional and artificial. In performance, it was another matter; Karsavina was evidently as bewitching as ever (the photographs of this ballet are among the most delightful pictures ever taken of her), but it was again Nijinsky who was the sensation of the evening.

Attention has been focused on his final leap from the stage through the open window of the room

Le Spectre de la Rose, *in which the choreographer, Fokine, imagined a girl half-asleep after a ball dancing with the spirit of a rose to the music of Weber's* Invitation to the Dance, *was created on Nijinsky and Karsavina – a couple whose partnership lifted it from a simple* pièce d'occasion *to an experience never forgotten by those who saw it.*

Revivals of Le Spectre de la Rose *have never caught the magic of the original ballet as danced by Nijinsky and Karsavina: only an artist of Nijinsky's extraordinary assurance could, even in 1911, have carried off an appearance in Bakst's very feminine costume of rose-petals – on the first night pinned to the costume, and occasionally to the dancer's flesh.*

Bakst designed for the piece. Just as on his first appearance in Paris, he rose from the boards to leave the impression that he soared away beyond the sight of the audience. Fokine later rather sneeringly observed that the sill of the window was only a foot above the ground, 'quite sufficient for Nijinsky's leap' – though he certainly jumped high enough to require a mattress to be placed in the wings on which he would land to lie breathless for a while before taking his calls.

Quite apart from this, however, accounts of the

Right *The artist Valentine Gross saw almost every performance of the Ballets Russes, sitting in the gallery and sketching the dancers; here, she shows Nijinsky and Karsavina in* Le Spectre de la Rose.

Nijinsky's great achievement in Le Spectre de la Rose *(1911) which no subsequent male dancer has matched, was to seem inhuman – not a man dressed in rose-petals pretending to be a flower, but the very spirit of the rose itself, all human movement and personality miraculously sloughed away.*

ballet suggest that he succeeded in creating an extraordinary, detached, almost scented aura – which incidentally must have been immeasurably helped by his make-up, which photographs show to have been creative and original, turning his face into an almost depersonalized shape, not unlike the petal of a flower, while his expression was somehow inhuman – smiling, but with a humourless sweetness which was strangely unnerving. He represented, the critic Jacques Riviere said, a faded flower too fragile to withstand even the inhalation of its own perfume.

The audience certainly approved of the ballet: even Fokine admitted that there was 'thunderous applause' as a matter of course each time Nijinsky made his dramatic exit – applause loud enough at the first Paris performance to drown the music; the orchestra could not complete the score. Diaghilev saw one woman faint. Critics suggested that Nijinsky's elevation was so prodigious that he must surely be permanently painted on the ceiling!

Perhaps the feat was not as spectacular as it seemed in the excitement of the moment. Stanislas Idzikowsky, the Polish dancer who joined Diaghilev in 1914, claimed that it was in the *length* of his leaps that Nijinsky was unbeatable – he himself, he said, could actually jump higher. And in any event, as Karsavina was to put it: 'Everyone always talks about his giant elevation and even wants to know how high it was – how many inches. One never thought of measuring it!' The real achievement was in the total performance. Vaslav danced the role, Fokine said, 'magnificently'; but went on to point out that the effect of the final jump was 'not due to the height of that leap – not at all – but to its being the termination of a most ethereal, light and poetic dance, immensely difficult to perform. . . .'

Nijinsky was able to project 'the spirit of the rose' to an almost alarming degree. Years later he told an interviewer in America: 'One has no sex, no

Spectre de la Rose: *Karsavina, as a young girl drowsy after her first ball, awaits the vision of the rose which will awaken her.*

form, in the girl's imagination ... [one is] a half-shaped dream, awaiting the breath of love to transform it into being.' No dancer since has been able to achieve that effect, or to wear with conviction any costume even slightly resembling the one Bakst designed – a pink leotard to which were sewn limp silk petals of pink, red and purple. Even Nijinsky, in the photographs of him in the role, looks faintly embarrassed.

It was now possible to spend time on the ballet on Greek themes which was increasingly preoccupying him (and which was very much a secret from everyone except his sister and Diaghilev). He had started rehearsing Bronia in *L'Après-Midi d'un Faune* in St Petersburg, working intensely on movements she found extremely difficult and original. She was extremely concerned at what Fokine's reaction would be to the news that Nijinsky was to be allowed to choreograph for the company of which he was Choreographic Director. Diaghilev too may have been worried, and perhaps for that reason told Vaslav that his ballet would not be mounted until 1912.

The one role of Fokine's Nijinsky had to learn for the new season was *Narcisse*, in which a Greek boy tried to teach Echo to dance, failed, and then

Nijinsky in Fokine's Narcisse, *a mythological subject in which he had little opportunity to shine – perhaps because the overt eroticisim necessary to a full realization of the role would not have been possible in 1911.*

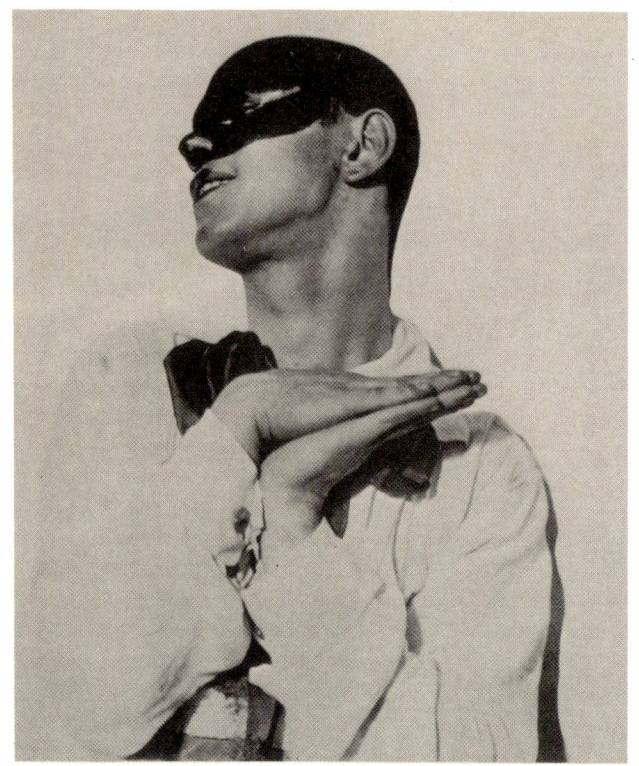

Nijinsky as Harlequin, in Carnaval, *was once more transformed: a mask covered the upper part of his face, emphasizing slant eyes which shone like those of a cat. Once again, he seemed to the audience to be inhuman, some animal miraculously endowed with a sense of humour.*

sank into the pool in which he saw, and loved, himself. It was not a success, though Nijinsky looked very fetching in a simple, loose, revealing white tunic, with bare limbs and in one photograph bare feet – something of an innovation in 1912. He looked, Bronia says, like Michaelangelo's David – though his body make-up was not white, like marble, but an unusual lemon-brown which gave him an air of unreality, accentuated by the fact that Bakst had insisted that he wear no facial make-up at all, only the lips being faintly outlined in pencil.

It is possible that the ballet's lack of success may have been simply because the theme was too daring for its time: it would clearly have been impossible to convey overtly the erotic sensuality of the part – though in London, Nijinsky's figure, Charles Ricketts said, aroused such interest that, 'Duchesses had to be led out of the audience blinded

Nijinsky first danced the role of Harlequin in Le Carnaval *in June, 1911, in Paris, and was much admired both by the public and the critics; his thin tight-fitting costume and tights revealed each muscle, and each muscle, Nijinska said, 'vibrated with joy'. She thought this role one of her brother's greatest achievements.*

with emotion, and with their diamond tiaras all awry.'

Early in February, the company arrived in Rome, and Diaghilev and Nijinsky settled into an hotel at the bottom of the Via Veneto. Their stay was extremely busy, for apart from performances at the Teatro Costanzi, the company was preparing *Petrushka*, *Sadko*, *La Peri* and *Le Dieu Bleu* for the Paris season, now only a month away. In an unventilated basement buffet at the theatre the atmosphere became so close that even the punctilious Stravinsky asked the ladies' permission to remove his jacket. The hard work took the edge off the season's success— though it was a success, at least partly because the King of Italy attended the first night and demonstrated his enthusiasm at *Le Pavillon d'Armide*. But the morning after the performance, the company was back in the theatre rehearsing *Petrushka*.

Meanwhile, frenzied letters and cables about the composition of the Paris programmes went to and fro between Diaghilev and Astruc. Finally, agreement – or rather compromise – was reached, and the company arrived in Paris for the first performance there, on 6 June at the Théâtre du Châtelet, of Les Ballets Russes de Serge de Diaghilev.

At the gala performance which opened the 1911 season, despite the romance of *Spectre*, the drama of Fokine's and Stravinsky's *Petrushka* and the exoticism of *Schéhérazade*, many balletomanes found the first Paris *Carnaval* the most miraculous offering of the Diaghilev ballet. Karsavina danced Columbine, Adolf Bolm was the tragic Pierrot, Cecchetti showed his mastery of mime as Pantalon and Nijinsky once again appeared as Harlequin – a part Vaslav made peculiarly his own. His costume was not one which would have appealed to the Maryinsky management, with its close-fitting tights and no breeches. Even Diaghilev insisted that

Nijinsky should wear trousers over them when the ballet was performed in London.

Marie Rambert remembered Vaslav as incomparable in this role: 'talk about twinkling feet! – like lightning, his feet went, and his pirouettes were swift; he was extraordinarily brilliant'. Jean Cocteau, though by this time rather irritated that Nijinsky did not return his admiration, described him in *Le Carnaval* as:

... an acrobatic cat stuffed full of candid lechery and crafty indifference, a schoolboy, wheedling, thieving, swift-footed, utterly freed of the chains of gravity, a creature of perfect mathematical grace. Desire, mischief, self-satisfaction, arrogance, rapid bobbings of his head ... and especially a way of peering out from under the visor of the cap he wore pulled down over his eyebrows, the way one shoulder was raised higher than the other and his cheek pressed against it, the way the right hand was outstretched, the leg poised to relax, such (and it was something never before granted me to see or hear at the theatre) was Vaslav Nijinsky in *Le Carnaval*, surrounded by an uninterrupted roar of applause.

Once more, it was Cyril Beaumont who left the most vivid impression:

Think of him one moment poised in an attitude of mockery, the next bounding and rebounding in the air with the ease of a bouncing rubber ball, or twirling round with the facility and precision of a spun wheel. All his movements were precisely timed; the gracefully extended hand with the beckoning finger; the impish mockery of his one big step to Columbine's dainty two, as they entered with their arms about each other's waists; then his thrilling solo with the *pirouette à la grande seconde*, ending in his unflurried sitting on the ground with crossed legs ... He did not so much as dance to the music, he appeared to issue from it. His dancing was music made visible.

After *Carnaval* there was a short interval, and during it members of the audience crowded backstage and into Nijinsky's dressing-room. Diaghilev was

Nijinsky dancing as Harlequin in Le Carnaval*, Paris, 1911.*

too aware of the importance of their good-will to attempt to exclude the fashionable, and Vaslav had to change his costume and make-up under twenty or thirty pairs of prying eyes. Vassili guarded him as well as possible, and Nijinsky protected himself by refusing to speak to anyone. Totally without self-consciousness, he stripped off his costume and applied his body make-up, concentrating single-mindedly on preparing for the next ballet, *Narcisse*.

A similar crowd watched as he put on the wig and costume for *Le Spectre de la Rose*, and on his soaring exit there was a roar. Yet it was the strangeness of the vision that captivated the more discerning: 'I shall never again smell a rose without this ineffaceable phantom appearing before me,' Cocteau exclaimed.

Orchestral rehearsals of *Petrushka* began with a minor revolt from the musicians, who burst out laughing at the score; Pierre Monteux, who conducted the first performance, had some difficulty in convincing them that they were not the objects of a practical joke. Even Fokine, it seems, did not care for the music. However, apart from that things went as smoothly as was possible with a large crowd of extras, each of whom had to be carefully drilled into giving an individual performance as a member of a crowd at a St Petersburg Fair. It was not easy: a peasant woman would appear roughly dressed but with the most elegant Parisian *coiffeur*; a Russian peasant wore a Spanish shawl; and, told to tie their heads up in kerchiefs, the women arranged them so that pretty kiss-curls hung fetchingly over their foreheads. Fokine raged, but since he raged in Russian, only provoked laughter from his French extras, which made him rage again.

It was on 13 June that *Petrushka* received its first performance. Again, Nijinsky previously danced in *Schéhérazade* and *Spectre* (as did Karsavina). Then came the now familiar story of the

Shrove Tuesday Fair in the bitter cold of a Russian winter; the Magician, Cecchetti, bringing his three life-sized puppets – the Moor, the Ballerina and Petrushka –to life with a touch of his wand; the scene in Petrushka's cell in which he tries to dance, is visited by the Ballerina, and dances out his frustrated love for her; a third scene in the Moor's cell, where he dances with the Ballerina, is futilely attacked by Petrushka and drives him away; and finally the last scene at the Fair, when the Moor kills Petrushka, who becomes a lifeless doll, sawdust bursting from his broken limbs. The crowd leaves, and as the Magician stands alone on stage, above him on the roof of his booth appears the spectre of Petrushka, waving his arms for a moment before slumping down on the tiles.

Fokine was again full of praise for Nijinsky's performance. Petrushka was, he thought, one of his finest roles: 'He grasped everything quickly and exactly, understanding thoroughly the purpose of each detail.' Grace Lovat Frazer, later to work for Diaghilev in London, felt that: 'he *was* a puppet, but he suffered, you knew that he suffered, you knew all his emotions – but that they were not the emotions of a human being, or of a human being pretending to be a puppet. And when he died, you didn't feel that there was anybody inside his clothes – it was just a heap of broken bits of wood and material. How he did it, I do not know.'

And again, Cyril Beaumont:

Nijinsky succeeded in investing the movements of his legs with a looseness suggesting that foot, leg and thigh were threaded on a string attached to the hip; there was a curiously fitful quality in his movements, his limbs spasmodically leapt or twisted or stamped like the reflex action of limbs whose muscles have been subjected to an electric current ... His features were made up a kind of putty colour, presumably a suggestion of wood; his eyebrows were painted out and replaced by a wavy line set half an

The single fact about Nijinsky's portrayal of the puppet, Petrushka, upon which everyone remarked was that he was not a dancer portraying a doll, but a doll which had miraculously come to life, and was impersonating a man.

inch higher; his lips were compressed together; his eyes boot-buttons or two blobs of black paint; there was a little red on his cheeks . . . He suggested a puppet that sometimes aped a human being, whereas all other interpreters conveyed a dancer imitating a puppet. He seemed to have probed the very soul of the character with astonishing intuition. Did he in one of his dark moods of introspection feel conscious of a strange parallel between Petrushka and himself, and the Showman and Diaghilev?

Osbert Sitwell always considered Nijinsky's Petrushka one of the most remarkable theatrical assumptions he ever saw:

I have seen other great dancers, but never one inspired as was Nijinsky; I have seen other great dancers play Petrushka, but never one who, with his rendering of a figure stuffed with straw, struggling from the thraldom of the puppet world towards human freedom, but always with the terrible leaden frustration of the dummy latent in his limbs, the movement of them containing the suggestion of the thawing of ice at a winter's edge, evoked a compar-

Audiences found it difficult to believe that the limbs of a great dancer were inside what seemed to be a sawdust-stuffed puppet, without muscles, whose arms jerked as though on wires. It was perhaps Nijinsky's masterpiece of characterization.

able feeling of pathos ... The part of Petrushka showed Nijinsky to be a master of mime, gesture, drama, just as, in pure dancing, his rendering of the Spirit of the Rose, in *Le Spectre de la Rose*, was the climax of romantic ballet.

The Paris season, a fairly short one, was the most successful yet. Nijinsky, by now fully in command of all his roles, had enough leisure to nurture his growing choreographic ambitions – doubtless encouraged by Diaghilev. His diary certainly strongly suggests that their relationship was by now under some strain – that the dancer had begun to resent the impresario's tight hold on him. Something of a puritan, he had been nauseated to see on the pillow traces of the dye Diaghilev used to keep his hair raven-black (except for a single lock of white over the forehead), and scorned his affectation of a monocle he did not really need.

'Left alone I ran after the girls,' he writes in his diary, suggesting that when he could escape from Daighilev's eye he used to spend his time walking the streets of Paris window-shopping for whores (and on at least one occasion, embarrassingly, being recognized while obviously following a *cocotte*). He claims that at this time he had as many as five girls a day (confident that he would not be infected, because the Parisian prostitutes underwent regular medical inspection). Diaghilev was presumably ignorant of these goings-on, for he was always on guard against the machinations of women attracted to Nijinsky. Vaslav once invited Maria Pilz, who danced the Chosen Maiden in *Sacre*, for a *fiacre* ride. As she was climbing into the carriage, she felt someone catch at her skirt. It was Diaghilev. 'Get out,' he said, 'you're not going anywhere with him.' Diaghilev, in fact, 'did not want me to do things alone,' Vaslav wrote, 'but I could not agree with him. We often quarrelled. I used to lock my door – our rooms were communicating – and would let in no one. . . .'

As the puppet in Petrushka, *Nijinsky had grey make-up, giving the impression that paint was flaking from his skin, and his face was painted to resemble that of a crudely-painted doll, its head lolling.*

Whatever inaccuracies afterthought may have put into Nijinsky's mind, he probably accurately recalled the strains which were developing, partly no doubt because he was not exclusively homosexual and was bored and intimidated by Diaghilev's friends and associates, many of whom – Proust, for one – found him dull and unintelligent. No one understood what was going on behind that blank face.

Off-stage, Benois, for instance, found him both physically and intellectually a cipher: 'a rather stocky man, not at all beautifully proportioned, and furthermore so timid that he seemed rather to fade into the background'.

Nijinsky as the puppet in Petrushka *which, with choreography by Fokine to a score by Stravinsky, and with Benois' décor, was one of the most memorable of the Ballets Russes' productions, and remains alive today.*

This had been the case, with him, since childhood. His stocky build, disproportionately muscular thighs, calves on which the muscles actually protruded ('like coiled springs'), and his apparent lack of capacity for intelligent thought, would have disqualified him from a place at the Imperial School had he not been transformed the moment he began to move, either in the classroom or on stage. To an extent he was entirely an instinctive dancer, knowing just how to execute the movements suggested to him by a teacher or choreographer, but incapable of verbalization – as he failed to be able to explain *Jeux*, later, to Karsavina. Fokine, choreographing some dances for *Acis and Galatea* in 1905, picked him out of the crowd of young extras, appearing as fauns, because the length and height of his jumps was so spectacular. But then, an onlooker noticed, he showed him not a movement but an intricate pose. Nijinsky instantly adopted it, ceasing to be a schoolboy and becoming a faun.

Gradually, of course, the necessity to appear in public under social rather than performing conditions gave him a degree of assurance – though, it seems, not much; and there is no doubt that his own ideas about the dance developed, and were sometimes openly expressed even in company he found intellectually inhibiting. A French journalist, Hector Cahusac, was once present when Daighilev, Cocteau, Bakst, Reynaldo Hahn and some others were sitting outside a café in the Bois during the 1912 season, discussing the development of the ballet. Bakst suggested that what was needed was a return to old balletic values, and Robert Brussel agreed: the charm of ballet lay in its being old-fashioned – and in any event how could modern ballet reflect in any way the most recent artistic movement, cubism? The human body was an instrument that could not be fragmented in that way.

Suddenly, Cahusac reports, Nijinsky came to

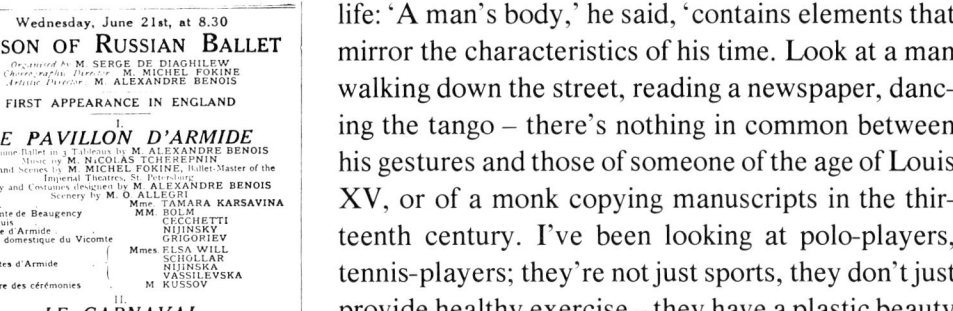

The programme presented at Covent Garden on the eve of the coronation of King George V. Several elderly ladies left the theatre during the 'barbarian horror' of Prince Igor, but the critic of The Times called the company 'the ideal dancers of the world'. Each of Nijinsky's jumps was 'a separate ecstasy', and in Carnaval he danced 'with incredible virtuosity'.

life: 'A man's body,' he said, 'contains elements that mirror the characteristics of his time. Look at a man walking down the street, reading a newspaper, dancing the tango – there's nothing in common between his gestures and those of someone of the age of Louis XV, or of a monk copying manuscripts in the thirteenth century. I've been looking at polo-players, tennis-players; they're not just sports, they don't just provide healthy exercise – they have a plastic beauty of their own, and we have to seek out forms which will characterize our own time just as expressively as the old ballet movements characterize the antique style of living and moving.'

An audience, Nijinsky continued, should not have to think while watching a ballet any more than one consciously had to think while looking at a painting or listening to music; he wanted to score a ballet so that its meaning would be the very movements in it – a bend of a finger, the stretching of a muscle – and not by mere jumps and pirouettes. . . .'

At this moment, the journalist noted, he stretched his arm up as though holding a tennis racquet, released his energy in a smashing drive towards a non-existent net, then turned his head as though following the flight of an imaginary aeroplane.

'Childish nonsense!' ejaculated Bakst; at which Vaslav relapsed into silence, and became again the anonymous figure most people remember – Lydia Sokolova, for instance, who never heard him express an original idea, but suspected that they were there, all the same.

In early June the company left for a London packed to the suburbs with visitors who had come for a sight of the celebration of the Coronation of George V. Diaghilev settled into the Waldorf (he later moved to the Savoy, which was to be his favourite London hotel); bookings for the dancers had been made at the Premier Hotel in Southampton

Row – a street the Russians found it almost impossible to pronounce, so that they were issued with cards bearing, on one side, their address, and on the other 'the Theatre Royal, Covent Garden'. Taxi-drivers apparently translated this as the Royal Opera House, where in fact they were to appear, alternating with evenings of Italian opera. They were also to contribute to the Coronation Gala there on 26 June.

A considerable amount of ballet, if in the form of short *divertissements*, was already available: Adelina Genée was at the Coliseum, Pavlova at the Palace, Catherine Geltzer at the Alhambra and Lydia Kyasht at the Empire. After a public dress rehearsal on 20 June, the Ballets Russes season opened on 21 June (the day before the Coronation) with *Le Pavillon d'Armide*, *Carnaval* and *Prince Igor*. Later came *Spectre*. Not only were the audiences enthusiastic, but the press was equally eager to praise the company – and to praise it thoughtfully and constructively. *The Sunday Times* particularly approved of Nijinsky:

He has great charm of personality: the grossness of contour and sensuality of lineament which so often mark the male dancer are conspicuous by their absence; and his every movement is instinct with spontaneity and grace. He seems to be positively lighter than air, for his leaps have no sense of effort and you are inclined to doubt if he really touches the stage between them. His precision is faultless and his technique generally as polished as it is resourceful.

Incidentally, as Nesta Macdonald discovered, it was on this occasion that the word *balletomania* seems first to have appeared in print in England – in the *Daily News* – though it was apparently in common use in Russia; later, Arnold Haskell was to coin the word *balletomane*.

There was another performance on 24 June before the Coronation Gala on 26 June, at which

The Ballets Russes' 1911 Coronation season in London attracted fashionable audiences, and was celebrated in the illustrated papers; the royal performance on 26 June included appearances by the singers Melba, Destinn, Kirkby Lunn, Tetrazzini, Malatesta and John McCormack, and the second scene from Le Pavillon d'Armide: *'Both the king and queen freely used opera glasses', said the* Daily Mail *(artist: Georges Barbier).*

Melba, Destinn, Kirkby Lunn, Tatrazzini, Malatesta and John McCormack appeared, and Karsavina and Nijinsky led the Diaghilev company in the *divertissement* 'L'Animation des Gobelins' from *Le Pavillon d'Armide.* The King and Queen bowed gravely from a royal box decorated with roses and orchids to an audience composed of all fashionable London – quite apart from the Aga Khan, who wore several strings of pearls, and oriental potentates in whose turbans sparkled enormous emeralds and rubies. Karsavina afterwards remembered that she was almost mesmerized by the flashing lights reflec-

Nijinsky, an inveterate doodler, sketched a character from Prince Igor *on a piece of Savoy Hotel notepaper, in 1911.*

ted from the jewels of her audience, and at one stage transfixed by the sight of a turbanned man in whose heavy beard sparkled several diamonds. Diaghilev spoke of 'muted applause' on this occasion: this was not because of any lack of enthusiasm, but because everyone was wearing gloves – the same reaction dampened the spirits of the singers at another Coronation gala performance forty years later, of Benjamin Britten's opera *Gloriana*.

While the company was in London its influence began to be felt: Cartier, the jeweller, produced a jewelled *collier à l'Armida*, and the most fashionable portrait-painter of the time, Sargent, sent for Vaslav and did a splendid drawing of his head and shoulders as the Favourite Slave.

After a summer holiday, the company was to give another short season at Covent Garden. Diaghilev meanwhile made a flying visit to Russia in an attempt to start negotiations for a season in St Petersburg. He was back in London in early October for the opening of the second season there, with Karsavina and Nijinsky in *Giselle*; and he brought news that Pavlova had agreed to appear in the ballet, at last, with Nijinsky.

As it turned out, it was rather a mistake to choose to open with *Giselle*; the public – even the critics (though there were few knowledgeable ones) – now regarded this as old-fashioned and tedious nonsense, and even the Pavlova/Nijinsky partnership, which Bronia, probably correctly, regarded as the positive apogee of the dancing of the time, went for nothing, while the sensational possibility of seeing Pavlova and Karsavina alternating in the role of Giselle seemed equally unattractive.

The reception of *Swan Lake*, with Nijinsky and Kchessinskaya, was equally unencouraging, and indeed does not seem to have been entirely without eccentricities. All of a sudden, and apropos of nothing Nijinsky ('radiant', as one newspaper put it, 'in cream, gold and orange, with peacock plumes waving in his hair') performed the interpolated dance of the Sugar Plum Fairy from *The Nutcracker*. *The Lady*, in a phrase which could perhaps have been better chosen, said that he was 'a vision of fairyland.'

Schéhérazade commanded the usual superlatives, as did *Carnaval*. Interestingly, Kchessinskaya (despite friction with Diaghilev) appeared also in *Giselle* and *Carnaval*, and in her memoirs, later, accused Vaslav of tearing his costume to pieces because he was so jealous of the applause she received from the Covent Garden audiences – a fairly obvious fabrication, though it is true that (partly as the result of a massive publicity campaign in the London press), her performances were rather better received than his. However, on the last night of the season, on 9 December, the audience applauded for twenty minutes, and Nijinsky was presented with a giant laurel wreath.

Some attempt was made during the season to woo Pavlova into joining the company, but dinner with Diaghilev at the Savoy Grill had no effect; and to Vaslav's suggestion that she could serve her art better as prima ballerina of the Diaghilev Ballets Russes than as a music-hall turn, she simply replied that she needed the money.

The day after the final performance, Diaghilev, Nijinsky and Bronia crossed the channel in a vicious storm: Diaghilev, always afraid of the sea, retired to his cabin before the ship left Dover, where Vassili produced an icon from among his luggage and spent the voyage praying for deliverance. Bronia was severely sea-sick; but Vaslav spent the whole time on deck, revelling in the storm.

Vaslav and Bronia went on to the Italian Riviera to stay with Diaghilev's friends, the twin brothers of Tchaikowsky, while Diaghilev remained in Paris to sign contracts for another season there before going off to supervize a season in Berlin. He was hoping also to organize performances in Amsterdam, Vienna and Budapest and a German tour. In Berlin he arranged for Mata Hari (later shot as a spy) to appear in Russia in the Ida Rubenstein role in *Schéhérazade*; and it was in that city that Fokine began rehearsals for *Le Dieu Bleu*.

There was continuing concern, all this time, about the probability that if he returned to Russia, Nijinsky would be liable for military service. Diaghilev had at first insisted that his influential friends would be able to square the Army and obtain a complete remission of the conscription; but it seemed more and more likely that the only solution would be to keep the dancer away from home.

Meanwhile, after a short Christmas season in Paris, the company spent January in Berlin, where – still in secret – Nijinsky began to reveal the choreography of *L'Après-Midi d'un Faune* to the company, rehearsing six members of the *corps* as the nymphs. He demonstrated the curious steps – in imitation of bas-relief – with ease, but the girls found them at first almost impossible to execute, and he frequently lost his temper with them. There was difficulty with Debussy's score, too, for the pianist – an excellent and professional musician – could not cope with the tempo Nijinsky wanted. Finally, when Ida Rubenstein appeared to run through the part of the chief nymph, she announced that it was impossible, and declined to play it. There was not a single natural movement in the piece, she said, and if she performed it she would dislocate every bone in her body.

The company was expecting to perform with or without Nijinsky at the Narodny Dom Theatre in St Petersburg, but before they left Berlin news came that the theatre had been burned to the ground. A short-notice tour to Dresden, Vienna and Budapest was arranged. It was not an especially happy tour: the company continued to be successful, but overwork was tiring Nijinsky, in particular, and the strain of secret rehearsals for his ballet contributed to a nagging illness which damped down his performances in Berlin and Vienna, where, unprecedentedly, he was unable to dance on the opening night.

It was in Monte Carlo, in March, that Fokine began to rehearse his new production *Thamar*. At the same time plans for *L'Après-Midi d'un Faune* came into the open, and formal rehearsals were announced – to the surprise and chagrin of Fokine, from whom the whole project had been kept secret; his anger was exacerbated when Nijinsky began to demand more and more time for rehearsals of his first full-scale choreographic effort.

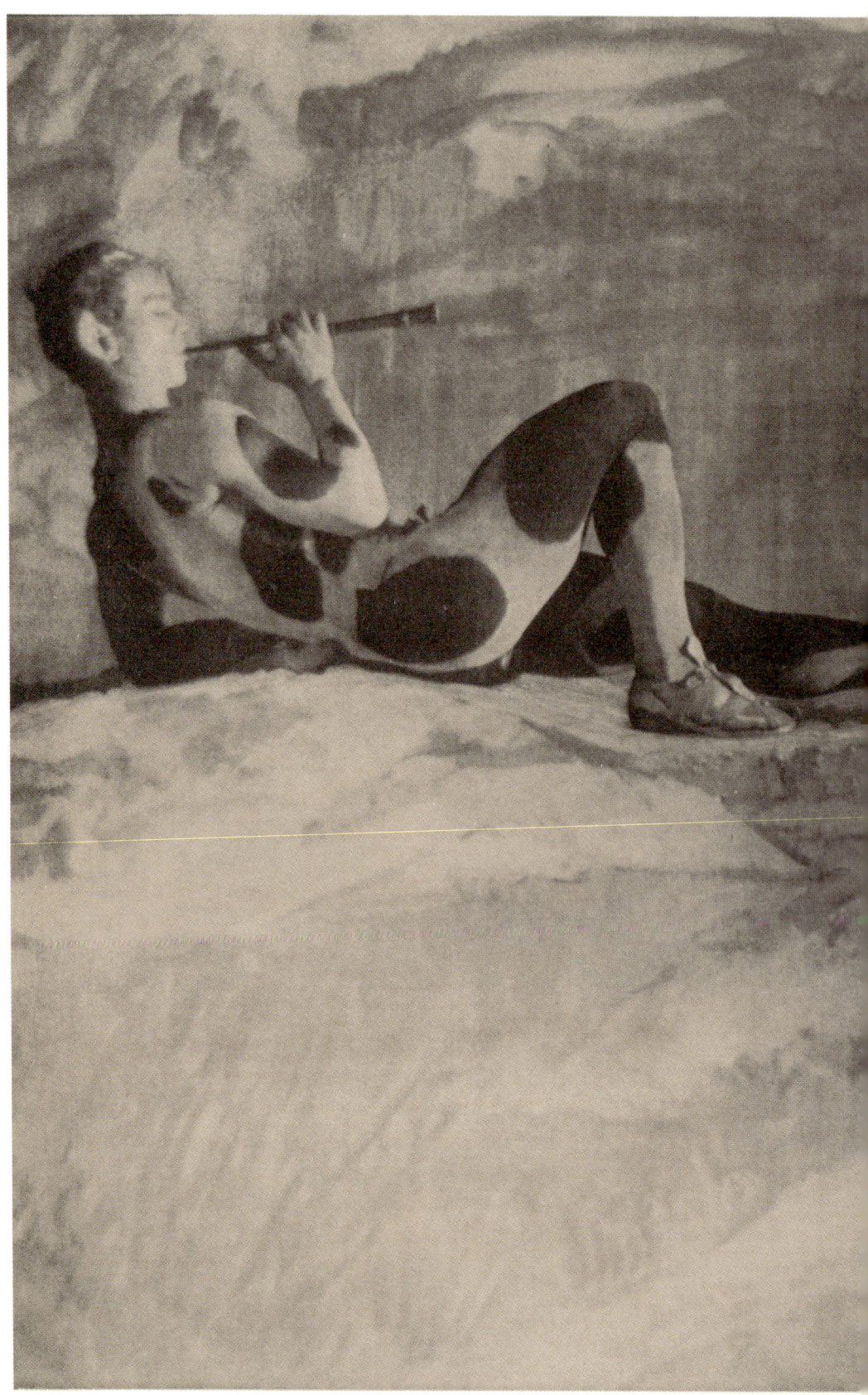

CHAPTER IV
The Choreographer 1911–1913

It had been during 1910 that Nijinsky, working in secret with Bronia, had started to devise *Prelude à l'Après-Midi d'un Faune*, inspired by a poem of Mallarmé. He first created the parts of the faun (which he was to dance) and the principal nymph on her, moulding her (she said) like a piece of clay. Diaghilev knew of the experiments and encouraged them; indeed, it seems to have been he who suggested the use of the Debussy music some time after Nijinsky had begun to conceive the unique style of the ballet, which was that of a Greek frieze thrown into movement – an idea suggested to him, Vaslav later claimed, by the Elgin marbles, bas-reliefs and Greek vases he saw in the British Museum.

Early in 1911, Diaghilev and Bakst were shown as much of the ballet as then existed. It related the adventures of a faun among nymphs; but rather than composing a ballet which would have enabled himself as the faun to show off his jumps and dexterity, Nijinsky was preparing a slow-moving, even static piece; he had invented no showy steps for himself, and the nymphs were to move with their bodies facing the audience but their faces in profile – and with bare feet. Diaghilev's immediate reaction is unrecorded; though he was certainly not deterred by the radical nature of the piece, he seems to have been uncharacteristically a little nervous of actually presenting it to the public, and its *première* was postponed – though he did ask Debussy's permission to use the music ('Why?' was the composer's unenthusiastic response).

The progress, the very existence, of Nijinsky's

Left *Critics often suggested that Nijinsky, in his ballets, was more animal than human, and in* L'Après-midi d'un Faune *this characteristic was certainly marked: in gestures, appearance, movement, he was the apotheosis of sleek, nervous, instinctive, sensual animal.*

ballet had been, at first, a close secret from everyone in the company. Early in 1912, the *régisseur*, Grigoriev, was told about it. The secrecy, he believed, was partly because Diaghilev wanted to be sure that the ballet would at least be producible, but also because he was afraid that Fokine – with whom relations had become rather strained – would walk out if he heard about it.

After the company had appeared in Budapest at the beginning of March, it returned to Monte Carlo to begin rehearsals for *Thamar*, a ballet for Karsavina and Bolm to the music of Balakirev. And now the trouble started, for Nijinsky wanted at the same time to rehearse his own ballet – and as well as a new principal dancer from Moscow, Lydia Nelidova, girls of the company were needed as nymphs. Fokine seized on every excuse for resenting Nijinsky's first venture into choreography. The new ballet would upstage his own *Daphnis and Chloe*, long delayed because of Ravel's slowness in completing the score; he would have less rehearsal time for *Thamar*; his position as the company's chief, nay only, choreographer would be usurped; and in any event, Nijinsky was in his opinion – though clearly a marvellous interpreter of Fokine's choreography – a musical illiterate, a man incapable of conveying his ideas clearly to anyone else, and obviously only being thrust before the public as a choreographer because of his special relationship with Diaghilev. Fokine announced that he would be resigning from the company as soon as *Daphnis and Chloe* had been presented.

The relationship between Fokine and the rest of the company became more and more uncomfortable. He quarrelled with Grigoriev over rehearsal time, was petulant with Diaghilev and short with Nijinsky; every man's hand, he believed, was against him. In a sense, he was right. Stravinsky, for instance, who had just completed the score of *Le Sacre du Prin-*

Off-stage, Nijinsky appeared almost conspicuously conventional, as in this studio portrait, which might be of a young businessman or clerk.

temps, told his mother that he was thoroughly depressed that Fokine, 'an exhausted artist', was to be its choreographer. 'New forms must be created, and the evil, the gifted, the greedy Fokine has not even dreamed of them.' Nijinsky, on the other hand, had certainly dreamed of new forms, and now, after no less than ninety weary rehearsals, had finally managed to teach his exhausted nymphs how to move in ways formerly unknown to classical dancers.

The company's antagonism to the strange new choreography never wavered, and it was only because of Nijinsky's single-minded determination and his meticulous manner of mounting the ballet that it ever came to the stage. He was exact in his planning: every movement made by every dancer to every bar of music was absolutely clear in his mind before he started formal rehearsals (unlike the method of many choreographers whose ballets grow in rehearsal, often with creative contributions from the dancers on whose bodies they are mounted). But the dancers still thought he was mad; those who were not appearing in the ballet would peer through half-open doors to sneer and predict disaster. Most of them felt that he should stick to dancing, and give way to Fokine as the company's established and successful choreographer. Even Diaghilev was for a time infected, and tried to persuade Nijinsky to re-think the entire work. Only Bakst struck a positive note: having seen a run-through, he embraced Vaslav, and told Diaghilev that the work was one of 'super-genius'.

On 13 May 1912, the fifth season of the Ballets Russes opened at the Théâtre du Châtelet, with *Firebird*, *Spectre de la Rose*, *Prince Igor* and *Le Dieu Bleu*. This last ballet, with a libretto by Jean Cocteau and Federigo de Madrazo and music by Reynaldo Hahn, was based on a Hindu legend, and Fokine in choreographing it had been influenced

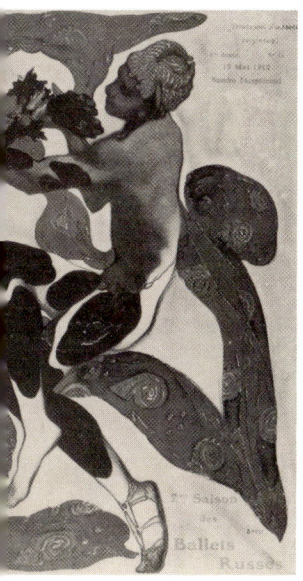

In his own L'Après-midi d'un Faune *Nijinsky wore all-over cream tights painted with brown markings like those of an animal; he had a short tail, and a wisp of vine-leaves around the waist, and two small golden horns on his head. The designs were by Bakst.*

once more by his memory of Siamese dancing. During a ritual celebration, a young novice was tempted by a priestess (danced by Karsavina); then a Blue God emerged from a temple pool to calm a number of threatening monsters, and after a magical display of posturing, promised peace.

The ballet was not a success, and was only performed for a short while; but it provides some of the most memorable images of Nijinsky as a stage personality – mainly due to the magnificence of the costume designed for him, as the Blue God, by Bakst. Indeed, Bakst's costumes and set designs were the single triumph of the ballet – they were among his most magnificent and successful. But the score was weak and derivative, and perhaps, too, Paris was tired of orientalism.

On 28 May despite Fokine's protestations, an invited audience attended a midday rehearsal of *L'Après-Midi d'un Faune*. The curtain rose on an almost abstract forest glade designed by Bakst; the backcloth was set so far forward on the stage that only narrow rectangular space was left in which the faun and nymphs moved, and this space was harshly lit so that the figures of the dancers in their long muslin tunics appeared to be in bas-relief rather than in three dimensions. Nijinsky wore tights and a close-fitting top which left his arms bare; his costume was covered with large brown spots so that he seemed to have the body of some strange animal.

To the audience's silent, almost stunned amazement, there seemed to be no dancing at all in the ballet – nor did the movements made by the dancers seem to have any relevance to the music, at least not in a sense demonstrated by any former choreographer. The flute certainly seemed to prompt or accompany the faun's movements, and there were certain climaxes in the score which signalled entrances or exits; but there was no matching of traditional ballet movements or gestures to traditional flourishes of

Right *Jean Cocteau wrote the libretto for* Le Dieu Bleu *(1912); the choreographer was Fokine, and for Nijinsky Bakst designed a costume in yellow watered silk, with bands of green velvet, yellow pantaloons, and many appliquéd stones. He wore a green make-up. Bakst's design was considered 'the zenith of decorative art'.*

Below *Bakst's costume for Nijinsky in* Le Dieu Bleu *was for some years on show in the amphitheatre foyer at Covent Garden; it has recently been withdrawn, and sold.*

music. Instead, the nymphs merely seemed to walk through the ballet, while Nijinsky moved with animal grace but also, it seemed, with as little conscious art as an animal. As the ballet opened, the faun sat on a bank playing his pipes, then squeezing the juice from a bunch of grapes into his mouth. The nymphs entered and moved about the narrow stage with what in 1912 may have seemed peculiar clumsiness. One of them removed her veil-like outer garment and, dressed in a simple gold tunic, bathed in the pool which evidently lay beneath the waterfall suggested in Bakst's backcloth. The faun came down from the bank, started to court the bathing nymph, was repulsed, picked up the veil she had dropped, played with it, laid it on the ground and lowered himself upon it as the curtain fell.

At the *répétition générale*, the silence in which

Right and overleaf
The relationship between the Faun and the nymphs in L'Après-midi d'une Faune *is clearly erotic, underlined by Debussy's languorous score, and it is not surprising that some people saw it as slightly obscene; on the other hand London society accepted it without a blink, and there was no suggestion of impropriety.*

L'Après-midi d'une Faune

the ballet was received persisted after its close; Astruc, after a moment or two, came before the curtain and announced that since it was such an unusual and difficult work, it would be performed again. This time there was more positive applause before the audience was invited into the foyer for champagne and caviare (an unprecedented event in the theatre of the time).

There was a much stronger audience reaction on the following evening, at the ballet's official first performance. The moment the curtain fell a mixture of booing and applause startled the company. It was the first time a Diaghilev ballet had received anything but approval. Whether to provoke further excitement or to comfort Nijinsky, Diaghilev ordered the piece to be repeated. This time, applause was more general; the great sculptor Rodin stood up in a stage box, shouting 'Bravo!', and Nijinsky took several curtain-calls as choreographer.

The press next morning was on the whole approving – with one startling exception, that of *Le Figaro*. Its ballet critic, Robert Brussel, was an enthusiastic supporter of the company and an admirer of Nijinsky; but spectacularly, the paper's editor, Gaston Calmette, declined to print Brussel's notice and instead himself thundered disapproval in a front-page article headlined *UN FAUX PAS*. 'We are shown', he said:

a lecherous faun, whose movements are filthy and bestial in their eroticism, and whose gestures are as crude as they are indecent. That is all. And the over-explicit miming of this mis-shapen beast, loathsome when seen full on but even more loathsome in profile, was greeted with the booing it deserved. Decent people will never accept such animal realism.

Diaghilev immediately sent off a reply, which *Figaro* published the following day. He quoted a letter from the artist Odilon Rédon congratulating Nijinsky on producing a ballet which would have delighted Mallarmé, and an article by August Rodin, published in *Le Matin*, in which the sculptor paid a striking tribute to Nijinsky's extraordinary success in portraying the wildness of a faun – apart from which he possessed the distinct advantage of physical perfection, with the beauty of an antique fresco or statue; he was the ideal model for whom every painter and sculptor had longed.

Calmette replied that Rédon did not know what Mallarmé actually thought of the ballet, since the poet was dead, and that as for Rodin it was time the state stopped paying a pension to a man who publicly exhibited indecent drawings to the swooning ladies and self-satisfied snobs who were his admirers.

The next few days saw the scandal swell and

Rodin, the great sculptor, leapt to Nijinsky's defence with a letter in Le Figaro *in which he compared Nijinsky in* L'Après-midi d'un Faune *to a figure in an antique fresco. Indeed, one of his purposes in the choreography is said to have been to present an animated scene which might have appeared on a Greek relief or vase.*

scatter. Political glosses were invented: Calmette was using the ballet as a pretext to attack French foreign policy, and it was the Franco-Russian alliance that was *Figaro*'s real target. Meanwhile, it was rumoured that the Parisian Prefect of Police was to stop further performances, and indeed police stood at the back of the theatre during the ballet's second performance on 31 May, though they took no action. There were, as far as could be seen, no empty seats in the auditorium on the second night, and the tremendous publicity the ballet received did not seem to result in any cancelled bookings.

There has been much discussion as to the real reason for the scandal. It has been suggested, and certainly seems possible, that Calmette seized on the ballet as likely to provoke a circulation-enhancing scandal. But clearly something about its ending genuinely shocked him – the faun's final movement before the fall of the curtain, when Nijinsky lay down on the veil dropped by the nymph; and it is clear that what he did was move his pelvis in a manner which suggested orgasm. There is no doubt that it was an overtly sexual gesture. Marie Rambert claimed that Nijinsky wanted to suggest the faun's first sexual experience. Some members of the audience noticed that at later performances Nijinsky, as he lay on the veil, placed his hands beneath him, thus suggesting masturbation as well as fetishism (one of Bert's photographs certainly bears this out). Calmette's implication that at some stage Vaslav exhibited an erection is unlikely enough to be absurd, but there is no doubt at all that there was enough in the last few moments of the ballet to scandalize the conventional, and even perhaps disturb the unconventional.

Fokine found it convenient to be outraged: 'One of the forms of sexual deviation was to be demonstrated in front of thousands of people. Why was this necessary? This was scandalous!' Yet at the ballet's first performance in London in 1913 it was

It was this final scene of L'Après-midi d'un Faune *(1912) that so outraged the editor of* Le Figaro, *who used the words 'filthy', 'bestial', 'crude', 'loathsome' and suggested that 'decent people will never accept such animal realism'.*

genuinely encored, as it was when Queen Alexandra saw it a few days later. Many critics found it entirely inoffensive.

The choreography has received more attention in retrospect than at the time. Contemporary critics did not seem to know what to make of it. Fokine's reactions, once he had cooled down, are particularly interesting. In the first place, he declined to refer to the dancers' movements as 'dancing' (it might be remembered that he was one of the most severe critics, later, of Martha Graham, and considered most developments in modern dance as calamitous). At the same time he accused Nijinsky of plagiarizing some of his own choreographic inventions (including the slow descent on the veil at the end of the ballet, which he claimed to have devised for the Venusberg scene in *Tannhäuser*, though then the dancer had lowered himself not onto a veil but onto a woman, which presumably he considered less offensive). But he did notice the originality of the running movements devised by Nijinsky, with the dancers moving not on the balls of their feet but placing the whole foot, heel first, on the ground; and he thoroughly approved of Nijinsky's use of stillness, courageously ignoring the music which suggested violent movement. And he thought that the 'archaic, angular choreography' suited the tone of the score.

L'Après-Midi d'un Faune continued to be difficult for the dancers of its time, used to the formal movements of classical ballet. They had to count their way through Debussy's score, for as Lydia Sokolova later recalled, though the audience and even the critics did not seem to notice the fact, each musical sound had its corresponding movement: as a dancer made her exit, she passed the counting of bars (as it were) to her colleague going on stage. Sokolova seemed to find the experience almost akin to going into a religious trance.

But at the centre of the ballet was Nijinsky himself, once more creating a role which no one else has ever danced entirely satisfactorily (Nureyev, in a brilliant recreation of the ballet based on the memories of Marie Rambert and others, has perhaps approached this most closely). Cecil Beaumont described Vaslav's performance in his *The Diaghilev Ballet in London*:

There was something cat-like about his propensity for indolence and the elasticity of his slow, deliberate, remorseless movements. His features were set and expressionless, and did not change throughout the ballet. By this means he suggested the brute, the creature actuated by instinct rather than by intelligence. Perhaps the most unusual characteristic of Nijinsky's portrait was this lack of emotion, all feeling being subject to the exigencies of pure form.

Sokolova found him thrilling in the role:

Although his movements were absolutely restrained, they were virile and powerful, and the manner in which he caressed and carried the nymph's veil was so animal that one expected to see him run up the side of the hill with it in his mouth. There was an unforgettable moment just before his final amorous descent upon the scarf when he knelt on one knee on top of the hill, with his other leg stretched out behind him. Suddenly he threw back his head, opened his mouth and silently laughed. It was superb.

Diaghilev must have been delighted with the publicity which followed the first night of *L'Après-Midi d'un Faune*. But it certainly overshadowed the

The artist Una Troubridge watched the Ballets Russes company classes at the Territorial Hall in Chenis Street, Tottenham Court Road, and later produced this bust of Nijinsky as the Faun – the only portrait head known to exist.

coming production of Fokine's *Daphnis and Chloe*, still barely completed. A combination of circumstances delayed its first night, and as the season was to end soon only two performances could be scheduled. Not unnaturally, this annoyed Fokine, already in a rage over an alleged lack of rehearsal time. He was even more outraged when he learned that Diaghilev had not only decided that *Daphnis and Chloe* should be performed first, rather than as the middle ballet of the evening, but had also decreed that the performance should start half an hour earlier than usual. He had a tremendous row with the impresario in the auditorium of the Châtelet, accusing him of turning the company into a degenerate pack of perverts, and describing his relationship with Nijinsky in very plain terms.

There was now no disguising the enmity between Diaghilev and Fokine. The company split into factions, some dancers siding with one, some with the other; Nijinsky was caught between the two – he greatly admired Fokine's work (which after all had provided him with his most successful roles) but had to be loyal to Diaghilev.

Even Fokine admitted that *Daphnis and Chloe* was perfectly performed, by friends and foes alike, at its première on 8 June 1912. Nijinsky and Karsavina danced the leading roles of the lovers, with Bolm as the rival cow-herd. After taking several curtain-calls with the principals Fokine left the theatre and dined alone with his wife. When they returned to their hotel they found a group of dancers waiting with flowers and a small gift. But when the company left for London Fokine was not with it. It was announced that he had severed all connection with the Ballets Russes.

No sensation was expected in London, and none occurred. Mr Thomas Beecham conducted *Thamar* and *Firebird*, which was on the whole well received – despite the fact that Beecham was never

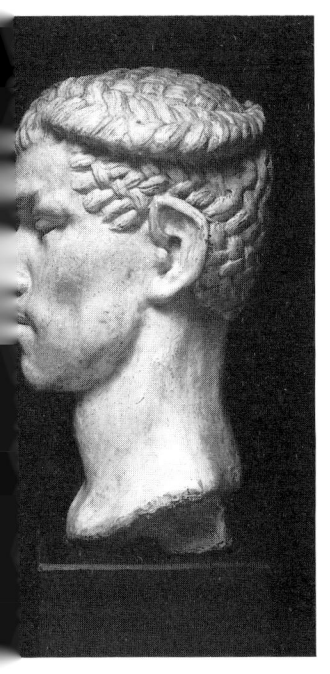

Una Troubridge's bust of Nijinsky as the Faun, lost for years, was rediscovered by Richard Buckle, holding open the door of a junk shop in London.

specially drawn to the ballet, and on one occasion, having conducted a score at a ridiculously quick tempo, was heard to mutter to himself: 'That made the buggers jump!'

Cecil Beaumont saw Nijinsky in *Les Sylphides*, and ever afterwards regarded him as the greatest of all male dancers: 'He danced not only with his limbs, but with his whole body, and the sequence of movements composing [the *pas seul*] flowed one into the other, now swift, now slow, now retarded, now increasing in speed, with a suggestion of spontaneity that had all the quality of music.'

The main event of the visit for the Nijinskys was Bronia's marriage, on 15 July in the Russian Orthodox Chapel of the Russian Embassy, to another member of the company, Sasha Kotchetovsky. Vaslav was best man, holding the gold crown above his sister's head during the ceremony. (Did he notice that the bride was wearing a ruby pin given to her, years ago, at her graduation from the ballet school, by his first patron, Prince Lvov?) There was a champagne reception at the Embassy, and later Diaghilev and Vaslav entertained the couple, with Liota and some friends, to supper at the Savoy, where Vaslav gave the Kotchetovskys a thousand roubles as a wedding present.

During this season Nijinsky was able to relax and enjoy his success; the strain of producing his first ballet was over, and he had to cope only with a familiar repertory – *Thamar* was the only work new to London. In his case it is difficult to know how far he actually enjoyed either his success or the company of the admirers it brought him. In Paris, one suspects that he found many of Diaghilev's intellectual friends as dull as they found him – though doubtless they stimulated his imagination. In London, the circle of people to whom he was introduced was a very different one. At Hanover Lodge, Regent's Park, he was fêted at a party thrown by Admiral and

Sir Thomas Beecham, preparing the score of Firebird *for the 1912 Covent Garden season, said it was the most difficult he had ever worked on; the composer, the following year, thought Beecham and his orchestra gave the finest performances of* Petrushka *he had yet heard.*

Mrs Beatty, attended by Prince and Princess Louis of Battenburg and Mr Winston Churchill. Lady Ripon gave another party at Coombe, and the Aga Khan threw one at the Ritz. The King and Queen, with the Grand Duke and Grand Duchess George of Russia attended the company's final performance.

The most prominent hostess to receive Diaghilev and Nijinsky was the extraordinary Lady Ottoline Morrell, the devoted friend (if also sometimes the butt) of the Bloomsbury set. Lady Ottoline, who at first had been doubtful whether any dancer could be quite as remarkable as her friends suggested, found Nijinsky's performances enthralling – 'Anyone who so completely lost himself and embodied an idea was not just a good ballet-dancer . . . he seemed no longer to be Nijinsky, but became the idea which he was representing.' Though when she was first introduced to him, she found him 'very quiet and rather ugly', she seems to have made rather a set at him. Lytton Strachey found them sitting together on a sofa, and overheard her pressing him about his theory of the dance: '*Quand vous dansez, vous n'êtes pas un homme – vous êtes une idée. C'est ça, n'est-ce pas, qui est l'art?*' Nijinsky, Strachey says, replied with an enigmatic grunt. And indeed most people found him extremely taciturn, not only because he knew no English – or rather only a few words, including 'Picadill' (useful no doubt if he got lost) and 'Littler', by whom he meant the celebrated Little Tich he so much admired.

Some people reacted to him, at first, very favourably. 'Nijinsky is very nice,' Strachey recorded, 'and much more attractive than I'd expected – in fact very much so, I thought.' But he added, 'otherwise, he didn't seem particularly interesting.' Strachey was of course homosexual, and was perhaps attracted to Nijinsky's physique, though that was not conventionally attractive, off-stage: in *Modern Dance Magazine*, an American journalist was to write of him, a few years later:

> He resembles a half-grown Cossack without a beard, and in New York he might pass for a shipping clerk or a plumber's apprentice... He looks like a rough person. He is about five feet eight inches, slim and angular; he has the small Slavic nose, small, black, almond-shaped eyes... prominent cheek-bones, a large mouth and narrow chin. His hands are big enough for a working man.

though another American journalist commented that:

> his charms appear to lie entirely in his figure. His face can hardly be an attraction, unless there are some women who love ugliness... He has the high cheekbones, the broad flat nose and the thick lips of the Mongolian race.

His personality was elusive; Sokolova thought of him as:

> himself like a faun – a wild creature who had been trapped by society and was always ill at ease. When addressed, he turned his head furtively looking as if he might suddenly butt you in the stomach. He moved on the balls of his feet, and his nervous energy found an outlet in fidgeting. When he sat down he twisted his fingers or played with his shoes. He hardly spoke to anyone, and seemed to exist on a different plane.

Lady Ottoline, who observed him as closely as anyone in England, thought that 'he seemed lost in the world outside, as if he looked on as a visitor from another world, although his powers of observation were intensely rapid. For on entering a room he would see all the pictures hanging in it before he had been there but a few minutes.' Occasionally, too, a touch of mocking humour showed itself. On one occasion Sir Osbert Sitwell was at dinner when Diaghilev embarked on an apparently interminable anecdote. As it ended, Nijinsky looked up from his place and observed succinctly: '*Histoire longue, mais pauvre.*' On another occasion he said of Ottoline, 'Lady Morrell is so tall, so beautiful, like giraffe.' Diaghilev politely demurred, thinking she would be offended, but Vaslav repeated: 'No, no, giraffe is beautiful, long, gracious – she looks like it.'

Nijinsky does not seem to have gone out alone into London (or any other) society: Lady Ottoline referred to Diaghilev as Vaslav's 'guardian and jailer'. His possessiveness had an element of self-interest, of course – not only because Vaslav was a very valuable property, but because he loved him. There is no evidence that the dancer felt as strongly for Diaghilev as the latter for him; indeed there is a hint that he enjoyed tormenting the older man, for Lady Juliet Duff recalled seeing the impresario weeping copiously at a party to which, after a disagreement, Vaslav had declined to accompany him. Wherever one of the partners in a homosexual affair is bisexual, there may well be a basic insecurity; and while it is certainly not true that (as some journalists, especially in America, were fond of suggesting) Vaslav was leading a spectacularly dissolute life amid a harem of beautiful, rich women, jealousy may already have been eating away at the relationship.

Nijinsky was already thinking about the ballet he had conceived some months ago, based on an exploration of the movements made by atheletes or sportsmen. It is said that one evening he and Diaghilev were walking with Lady Ottoline through the gardens of Bedford Square, and came upon Duncan Grant and Adrian Stephen (Virginia Woolf's brother) playing tennis in the dusk. Vaslav watched their athletic young bodies moving against the gloom of the trees, and exclaimed, '*Quel décor!*' It seems the most reliable account of the final genesis of *Jeux*, even if (as he suggests in his diary) the general idea had been put into his mind by Diaghilev some time previously.

After the close of the London season, there were performances at Deauville, to open the new Théâtre de Casino there. Liota left Vaslav and Bronia to return to St Petersburg, where there had been a *rapprochement* of sorts with Foma, and where Stassik was now hopelessly mad and permanently incarcerated. Vaslav, still unable to return to Russia, made a short expedition to Bayreuth with Diaghilev and Stravinsky to hear *Parsifal*, and then made for Paris, where he was to hear the score Debussy had produced for *Jeux*, and where he had also promised to pose for Rodin. The sculptor worked with the dancer for some time, making many sketches of him, naked, in a pose rather like that of Michelangelo's David. He was fascinated by Vaslav's musculature – the enormously developed thighs and upper body, yet the tiny waist – only sixty-three centimetres – and the slender dancer's neck. Diaghilev, from the first, seems to have been jealous of the intimacy which naturally developed between the dancer and the sculptor (who in fact was almost ostentatiously heterosexual), and after, one day, entering the studio, he found his lover and Rodin asleep, Vaslav covered only with a shawl, he seems to have managed to put an end to the sittings. Only a few small *maquettes* survive from the experiment, and some of them of doubtful provenance.

In September, after a short holiday in Venice, Nijinsky was in Monte Carlo ready to start rehearsals for *Jeux* – at first just with Bronia alone, and without even a pianist – his perfect musical memory enabled him to start choreographing the ballet without the score, which he had heard once, in Paris. There were only three participants, himself and two girls – to be danced by Bronia and Karsavina – though since the latter was at present at the Maryinsky, Alexandra Vassilievska was taking her place. Vaslav took both dancers with him to watch the tennis-players on the courts at Monte Carlo, and spent hours attempting to translate the movements he saw there into more formal balletic gestures.

Even to Bronia, the choreography again seemed strange and new, and Vaslav never gave her any idea of a libretto. In his diary he suggests that the ballet reflects a sexual fantasy of Diaghilev's: 'He wanted to have two boys as lovers. He often told me so, but I refused. Diaghilev wanted to make love to two boys at the same time, and wanted these boys to make love to him. In the ballet, the two girls represent the two boys, and the young man is Diaghilev. I changed the characters, as love between three men could not be represented on the stage.' It is fair to say that no inkling of this could have conveyed itself to an audience.

It was some time yet before the première of *Jeux*, however, and in the meantime rehearsals were interrupted by performances in Cologne – where just before *Schéhérazade* Vaslav received news of the death of his father. They organized a memorial Mass in Cologne Cathedral: Diaghilev supervised the music, and the whole company attended to commemorate the death of a fellow-dancer. They then travelled on to Frankfurt, Munich and Dresden – and deprived of the opportunity of continuing to rehearse *Jeux*, Vaslav turned his attention to another new project, the setting of Stravinsky's score, *Le Sacre du Printemps*, or *The Rite of Spring*.

The original conception of the ballet was probably that of Nicholas Roerich, the designer who had provided the décor for the *Polovtsian Dances*, back in 1909. He was also an eager amateur archaeologist, and in an interview in a St Petersburg newspaper had described his idea for a ballet which would consist of ritual dances performed before sunrise on a summer's night, and which would be 'the first attempt to reproduce antiquity without any explicit story'.

The ritual dance became the fulcrum of the second scene of the ballet, the *danse sacrale*, and Nijinsky began to choreograph it with Bronia as the Chosen Maiden. He and Bronia soaked themselves in the music, and she was by now so accustomed to her brother's choreography and manner of working that she did not find it difficult to interpret his ideas. Others were to find this less easy.

At the beginning of 1913, two women joined the company. The first was Miriam Ramberg, a student of Jacques Dalcroze's system of musical exercises, with which Diaghilev had been impressed on a visit to the Dalcroze Institute near Dresden. 'Eurhythmics', as the exercises were called, seemed to him to be likely to help his company to cope with the difficult rhythms of *Le Sacre du Printemps*, and he engaged Mlle Ramberg to help Nijinsky teach it to the company. She was later to be better known as Marie Rambert, founder of the Ballet Rambert.

Valentine Gross' impression of Nijinsky as the crumpled puppet, Petrushka.

'Rhythmitchka', as Rambert was known, was not, at first, a great success – as might indeed have been expected; the Dalcroze system was essentially anti-balletic. The company simply declined to attend her classes, which were soon discontinued. But she soon won her new colleagues around by the hard work with which she trained to become a competent member of the *corps*. When the completed orchestral score of *Le Sacre* was ready, and rehearsals started at the Aldwych Theatre in London (during the Covent Garden season of Spring, 1913) she was able to make herself useful to Nijinsky, helping individual dancers with their roles.

Petrushka and *Le Dieu Bleu* were greeted with only muted applause in London, but *L'Après-Midi d'un Faune* was received with enormous enthusiasm – so much so that at the first performance it was encored, as it was on the later evening when Queen Alexandra saw it. The only unusual incident that Spring – and there is no proof that the incident really did happen – was recalled years later by the former porter of a Poor Law Institution in the building which is now St Stephen's Hospital in the Fulham Road, where vagrants were offered a bed for the night. One

Right *The role of the god in* Le Dieu Bleu *should have been one of Nijinsky's great successes, and Fokine believed that he was never more marvellous than in this ballet. But it never pleased either critics or public.*

Below *Karsavina as the Doll in Fokine's* Petrushka *(1911), a role she created. Fokine, while he could never analyse her success in the role, insisted that no subsequent dancer equalled her in it.*

evening, he said, a young man was admitted in what seemed to be a drunken condition. He was put to bed, but the inmates of his ward were somewhat surprised when, the following morning, they saw him leap over the beds, doing the splits in mid-air, before he was collected by an elegant gentleman who shed sovereigns like confetti. The name of the inmate, set down for the records, seemed to be V. Nijinsky. There is no documentary evidence at all for this story, which used to be told and re-told by an ex-Mayor of Kensington – but he and his wife certainly repeated it often enough to have constructed a persuasive myth.

The second newcomer to the company was a

seventeen-year-old society girl, the daughter of the founder and director of the National Gallery of Hungary and Emilia Markus, the country's most distinguished actress. Her name was Romola de Pulszky.

She had seen the Diaghilev company in Budapest. On the first night on which she attended a performance, Nijinsky did not dance; determined to see the whole company, she went again, and like the rest of the audience was overwhelmed by the lively beauty of his Harlequin in *Carnaval*. Through her mother she managed to contrive an introduction to Adolf Bolm and to meet some other members of the company – but not Vaslav.

Though she had been training as an actress (under the great Réjane), she now decided that her future lay in the ballet, and when the company returned to Budapest, she attended class, went to every performance, and almost every rehearsal. She was introduced to Nijinsky by a newspaper reporter; he took her for the prima ballerina of the Hungarian Opera, which was not an advantage, as after discovering his mistake he henceforth ignored her. This did not dissuade her from pursuing him, which she did with well-planned enthusiasm. Though off-stage he looked, she said, like a Japanese student in ill-fitting European dress, there were also his almond-shaped, dark brown eyes, his extraordinary physique, his natural elegance and charm ... these, and his fame, entranced her.

Only old Cecchetti realized what was going on: 'Beware!' he whispered to the girl one day before rehearsal – 'Nijinsky is like a sun that pours forth light but never warmth.'

Romola realized, unconsciously no doubt, that the last thing she should do was allow Diaghilev to realise she was in pursuit of Vaslav; so she allowed the company to assume that there was a budding relationship between her and Bolm – and that her real ambition was to become a dancer. She even contrived a meeting with Diaghilev and persuaded him to arrange private lessons with Cecchetti. She could join the company in London in February.

For the moment, Nijinsky had no time for her, or for anything else but rehearsals for *Sacre*, which continued when the company returned to Monte Carlo after the London season. If the movements in *L'Après-Midi* had been unusual, those he invented for *Sacre* were even more so, and the dancers had the utmost difficulty in performing them, especially to Stravinsky's music, with its violently changing emphasis and rhythms.

The intention of the ballet was to show a primitive society in flux, prehistoric men and women celebrating the breaking of icy winter into the promise of spring in a series of orgasmic dances of the utmost violence and originality. The movement and postures of the dancers reflected their primitive nature: legs and feet were turned inward rather than outward, fists were clenched, shoulders hunched, movements clumsy and inelegant. So original was the choreography, so difficult the score, that there were a

Some of the dancers in Le Sacre du Printemps *(1913). Second from the right is Miriam Ramberg (Later Marie Rambert).*

hundred and twenty rehearsals before the first performance; and these were in themselves intensely traumatic for everyone.

Nijinsky was evidently determined to try for something entirely new: he was bored to tears with prettiness. Some years later he said in an interview in America: 'Really, I begin to have horror of the very word ["grace"]; "grace" and "charm" make me feel sea-sick ... The fact is, I detest conventional "nightingale-and-roses" poetry; my own inclinations are "primitive".' So his new work was to be about 'the life of the stones and trees. There are no human beings in it. It is the incarnation of Nature – not of human nature.'

By all accounts, rehearsals of *Sacre* must have been terrifying. The physical contortions Nijinsky demanded, so different from the movements of conventional ballet, confused the dancers. The members of the company must have felt they were on the rack: apart from having to discard the ideas of a lifetime, they had to put up with the strictest discipline, for Nijinsky would allow no latitude in the interpretation of his choreography; every movement had to be exact, precisely as he set it. He also expected the men to be able to leap as high and as far as he could, which was patently impossible. This all made for tension, as did the fact that Vaslav, who so rarely attended company class, and was more often in Diaghilev's company than that of his fellow-dancers, found it difficult to establish a rapport with them.

There was trouble with Stravinsky, too. Ridiculously, he treated Nijinsky as a musical clown, entirely incapable of realizing his score. In an interview given in 1936, he said: 'The poor boy knew nothing of music. He could neither read it nor play any instrument. The lacunae were so serious that his plastic vision, often of great beauty, could not compensate for them . . .' Stravinsky should have known better; Ravel could have told him of Vaslav's musical talent. But there was what Marie Rambert described as 'an epic quarrel' between Stravinsky and Nijinsky about tempo. Finally, there was a family upset when Bronia was discovered to be pregnant and had to withdraw from *Sacre* and *Jeux*. Valsav looked on this as a personal betrayal.

Jeux seemed mild as milk compared to *Sacre*; and of course fewer dancers were concerned. Whatever the true origin of the theme of the ballet, there did seem to be a highly charged sexuality about it – though this escaped the notice of the critics when it was first performed at the Théâtre des Champs-Elysées in May, 1913.

This season marked the opening of the theatre, for the façade of which the sculptor Emile-Antoine Bourdelle had provided a bas-relief inspired by the single occasion on which Nijinsky and Isadora Duncan had danced together (at a *soirée* in Paris in 1912). Though he did not care for her dancing, Vaslav had become something of a friend of Isadora, and was deeply affected by the tragedy of the drowning of her two children, not long before the season opened.

The significance of the choreography of *Jeux*, which was highly free and original, went unnoticed at its first performance. Both Karsavina and Ludmilla Schollar (who replaced Bronia as the other girl in the piece) had also found it difficult to grasp the significance of what Vaslav was attempting. The highly intelligent Karsavina later confessed that she was confused by the fact that Nijinsky could not explain the significance of the movements he asked her to make, but simply wanted her to parrot them. (But what modern choreographer has ever been able to 'explain the significance' of the movements?)

To Debussy's wonderful score – which must have seemed 'undanceable' in its time – two young girls and a young man moved in modified tennis clothes against a backcloth by Bakst vaguely suggesting a summer garden. Madame Paquin had made

Nijinsky, flanked by Tamara Karsavina and Ludmilla Schollar, in his ballet Jeux *(1913), based on a game of tennis, but really about human relationships; as Richard Buckle has pointed out, the poses chosen for photographs of this lost ballet emphasize a sculptural quality.*

the girls' white summer dresses, and Bakst's costume for Vaslav (which had originally included a red wig and knee-length trousers with red braces!) was modified by Diaghilev so that it eventually consisted simply of a white shirt and red tie, the trousers gathered just above the ankle. As the ballet began, in the one leap he allowed himself, Nijinsky, racket in hand, crossed the stage in pursuit of a ball. Then came the two girls, watched by Vaslav from behind some bushes. He flirted with one while the other jealously looked on,

142

then turned to the second; she comforted her neglected rival, and the three made a final tableau before a tennis-ball bounced on-stage, startling them, and they broke and fled.

Sokolova felt that, 'Nijinsky's idea must have been to turn his dancers into puppets by inventing a stiff and angular choreography, and to suggest that in the twentieth century love was just another game, like tennis . . .' Debussy cordially disliked the ballet, and so did several critics. The public, on the whole, was indifferent. It is impossible to judge, at this distance and on the evidence only of the two or three photographs which exist, but one has a sneaking suspicion that a modern audience might find this the most sympathetic of all Nijinsky's ballets.

Two weeks after the first night of *Jeux* came the first night of *Le Sacre du Printemps*. It is a legendary night in the history of twentieth-century theatre. The house was crowded, and excitement was high. By now, after innumerable rehearsals, the company was confident – and even perhaps lulled into a sense of false security. The dress rehearsal went like a dream, without any problem with either orchestra or dancers. But the moment the curtain rose and the first chords of Stravinsky's revolutionary score were heard, there was an uproar. Backstage, Marie Rambert recalled: 'As the music started there was already an incredible noise in the audience – we couldn't hear the music, we couldn't count; Nijinsky was counting wildly in the wings, I was counting on the stage . . .'

The dancers managed to continue, but the audience seems to have paid little attention to what was going on on the stage. People leaned from boxes to strike others because they were applauding; in the pit some were striking their neighbours because they were *not* applauding. The house lights were turned up and the clamour subsided for a moment: '*Je vous en prie – laissez s'achever le spectacle!*' cried Diaghilev from his box; then the row broke out again.

Nicholas Roerich, the designer of Le Sacre du Printemps, *worked closely with its composer, Stravinsky, and produced simple embroidered smocks which emphasized the ballet's association with ethnic, folk culture.*

The police were summoned during the break between the first two scenes, but could do nothing.

When the curtain rose for the second scene on a group of trembling girls with their hands pressed to their cheeks (trembling, it must be said, as instructed by the choreographer rather than because of their reception) someone cried, '*Un docteur!*' '*Un dentiste!*' cried another; and a third, '*Deux dentistes!*' A society woman spat at an applauding man; another slapped the face of a man in a neighbouring box, who was hissing. The Comtesse Réné de Pourtales rose, covered in diamonds, to accuse everyone of making fun of her, and swept from the theatre. Nijinsky's mother fainted. In the orchestra pit, Monteux continued imperturbably to conduct. Diaghilev climbed from his box to the top of the gallery, whence he shouted to the dancers to continue ...

It must have seemed, to them, a very long evening. Nijinsky climbed down from a chair upon which he had been standing, in the wings, shouting out the tempo to the dancers, and changed from practice clothes into his costume for *Le Spectre*, which he danced while the already exhausted *corps* put on their costumes for *Prince Igor*, which followed. Then, as the audience dispersed, Vaslav, Diaghilev, Stravinsky and Cocteau, to calm themselves, drove around the Bois in a *fiacre* until early morning.

Next morning, *Le Figaro* accused Nijinsky of pulling the public's leg; *Le Révue Française de la Musique* spoke of epileptic fits, absurd dancing, 'a choreography of puppets on strings'; *Le Monde Musical* found the piece 'oddly impressive', though 'grotesque and absurd'; and *Commédia* underlined the artist's right to experiment. The three further performances of the ballet during the Paris season were watched in polite silence, and though there were a few cat-calls it was at least tolerated. Significantly, Diaghilev told Stravinsky, after the first night, that the reception was 'exactly what I wanted'. And

The fashion designer Paquin designed the dresses worn by Karsavina and Scollar in Jeux; Nijinsky wore white shirt and trousers and a red tie. The ballet, though the photographs look cool and unemotional, evidently had a strong emotional charge.

indeed the publicity had been considerable.

The company now travelled to London. At Victoria station, Diaghilev was mildly surprised to see Vaslav raise his cap to Romola de Pulszky as she stepped from the train (she had managed to spend much of the journey chatting to him – or rather at him, since she spoke no Russian and he did not understand her French).

For the first time the company danced at the Theatre Royal, Drury Lane, and there *Jeux* (renamed *Playtime*) was performed. There was some laughter (chiefly at the size of the tennis-ball, which was more like a football) but though *The Times* thought the ballet resembled a language in which the speaker had restricted himself to a portion of the alphabet, the *Observer* found it 'full of perverse charm and fascination'. On 11 July *Le Sacre du Printemps* received its first British performance, to some laughter, some hissing – Nijinsky, in a *Daily Mail* interview said wryly that, 'people who say the piece was hissed cannot know what real hissing is!' – and some applause.

The press, similarly, was divided: the *Daily Telegraph* spoke of 'a whirlwind of cacophonous, "primitive" hideousness', and the *Standard* of 'bizarrerie and astonishing ugliness – ugliness on the stage and in the orchestra'. *The Times*' ballet critic was a great deal more discerning:

What is really of chief interest in the dancing is the employment of rhythmic counterpoint in the choral movements. There are many instances, from the curious mouse-like shufflings of the old woman against the rapid steps of the men in the first scene to the intricate rhythms of the joyful dance of the maidens in the last. But the most remarkable of all is to be found at the close of the first scene, where figures in scarlet run wildly round the stage in a great circle, while the shifting masses within are ceaselessly splitting up into tiny groups revolving on eccentric axes ... It is in this direction that [Nijinsky's] theories on ballet are capable of indefinite expansion.

Discussion of Nijinsky's most ambitious ballet, which only received a handful of performances and exists now only in the words of those who described it, has gone on almost interminably. One can only weigh the opinions of enthusiasts against those of antagonists, and attempt to reach a balance. Lytton Strachey was alone in being bored: 'I couldn't have imagined that boredom and sheer anguish could have been combined together at such a pitch.'

It seems most likely that *Sacre* was on no level completely successful; but at least it sounds inexhaustibly interesting, and Nijinsky certainly once more invented an entirely new language of the dance – dancers were asked to hurl themselves into the air not gracefully, but as though they positively hated the ground. They were to flop back to earth heavily, not with the ambition of landing ethereally, lightly, soundlessly. Even Diaghilev felt that there was no 'real dancing' in the ballet.

But *pace* Stravinsky, Nijinsky managed to find a movement or grouping for every musical phrase, even for each new piece of orchestration – as when in the first scene a group of girls in vivid scarlet huddled

Above *Nijinsky was eager to reject out-moded forms of the dance and to introduce symbols of the twentieth century:* Jeux, *in 1913, was based on a game of tennis, and was performed in sports clothes.*

Left *Stravinsky, among others, denied Nijinsky's musicality; but his concentration as he attempts the score of* Daphnis and Chloe *with the composer Maurice Ravel suggests that he was at least competent.*

together to the accompaniment of trumpet chords, for instance. And if Fokine, among others, was to claim that Nijinsky's only large-scale ballet 'led nowhere', at the very least it must be said that it loosened – nay, finally broke – the bonds of classicism, and so matched Stravinsky's musical effect. After the third London performance, *The Times* said that composer and choreographer had 'achieved something that, in spite of its defects, is a step nearer to a real fusion of music and dancing'. And at the very end of his life, Stravinsky told Yuri Grigorovich, the choreographer of the Bolshoi Ballet, 'Of all the interpretations of *Sacre* that I have seen, I consider Nijinsky's best.' It is a pity he was not a little more generous at the time.

There was one more London performance of *Sacre*: the seventh since its Paris first night. Then it was seen no more, and when Diaghilev wanted to revive it in 1920, no one could remember the choreography. Not only did that ballet die at the end of the 1913 London season; when the company dispersed for a short holiday before a South American tour, Vaslav Nijinsky had danced for the last time in England as a member of the Diaghilev Ballet.

Jean Cocteau caricatured Stravinsky at rehearsal for Sacre du Printemps, *confused and disgruntled dancers in the background.*

CHAPTER V

The Fallen God 1913–1950

On 15 August 1913, Diaghilev's Ballets Russes sailed from Southampton on the *SS Avon*.

Romola had been beside herself when she heard of a proposed South American tour. During the London season, by dint of simple perseverance – of always managing to place herself in his sight-line, at class, at the Savoy for dinner, in the theatre – she fancied that she was beginning to make some headway with Nijinsky; but now they were to be parted.

Happily for her, the company as a whole was extremely unenthusiastic about the tour, and so many members of the *corps de ballet* dropped out that Cecchetti suggested to Diaghilev that she should be formally engaged, despite the fact that even Romola herself knew she was not yet really ready to appear on stage. The only drawback was that there was to be no salary – simply a second-class ticket on the boat. Well, that was no real problem; the family had money, and she easily persuaded her parents to exchange the second-class ticket for a first-class one.

The passenger list for the *Avon* contained the names of Mr Vaslav Nijinsky (Deck A, Cabin 61) and Mr Sergei de Diaghieff (62). In fact Vaslav joined the boat at Cherbourg without his lover, whose fear of the sea finally overcame any motive he had for travelling with the company. It was the first time for years that he had been parted from Nijinsky. The parting was to be fatal for him – in a sense perhaps for them both. Romola, of course, was delighted as she saw Vaslav come up the ladder dressed in a smart travelling-coat and hat, but without his familiar.

Nijinsky and his wife Romola, photographed not long after their marriage.

Members of the company were surprised to find this non-dancer suddenly one of them, and various explanations began to suggest themselves. Romola's explanation (given in her biography of Vaslav) has seemed to some biographers to be too simple; they have suggested that Baron Dmitri de Gunsburg, placed in charge of the company by Diaghilev, had a hand in her presence. Diaghilev later seems to have believed that Gunsburg wanted to lure Vaslav away in order to form a company around him, and used Romola as bait. It does not seem likely, though certainly the Baron could not have been unaware of the effect on the impresario of a liaison between Vaslav and her – or indeed, any woman.

Vaslav's heterosexuality had never been entirely suppressed, and a three-week sea-voyage promoted just the atmosphere for flirtation. The other dancers soon noticed that though at first he spent his time alone, reading in a deck-chair, always neatly dressed in a light-weight suit or in white flannels, he soon seemed to be admiring Romola's beauty and elegance. When the company's new conductor, Rhené-Baton, lumbered up to her one morning and took her hand in his massive paw, Vaslav was heard to cry in his pigeon French: *'Peux toucher – pas casser!'* He allowed her to watch while he worked with Rhené-Baton on an abortive Bach ballet he had been planning with Diaghilev during what were to be their last days alone together, in Baden-Baden, just before he sailed; though broken French was the only language in which he and Romola could converse, they appeared to be discussing books and ballet.

If one is to trust Romola's account, all this was not achieved without considerable hard work. She walked endlessly round and round the deck, in order to pass again and again the corner where Vaslav was exercising; she ingratiated herself with a Mr Williams, an English masseur who was travelling with the company especially to look after Vaslav (he told her,

Nijinsky on board the SS Avon, *sailing from Europe to South America; it was during this voyage that, through an intermediary, he proposed marriage to Romola de Pulszky.*

incidentally, that the dancer's muscles were so strong that even an hour working on his body completely exhausted him). She would make a point of laughing or talking loudly whenever she was near Nijinsky, in order to make him notice her. It all sounds a recipe for disaster – but as the *Avon* approached Rio de Janeiro, Gunsburg came up to Romola as she sat in the bar, and asked to speak to her alone. 'Romola Karlovna,' he said, 'as Nijinsky cannot speak to you himself, he has requested me to ask you in marriage.' She said later that she thought he was making a cruel jest, and ran to her cabin to lock herself in. This was somewhat disingenuous. At all events, later that evening she ventured on deck, and Nijinsky himself, appearing from nowhere, pointed to his ring finger and said: '*Mademoiselle, voulez-vous, vous et moi?*' '*Oui, oui, oui!*' she replied.

The company was amazed at the news. One of the dancers congratulated Romola with the words: 'Unbelievable! But somehow I always knew Vaslav is not as people say!' (Then, realizing what she had said, she added: 'I mean, I am glad for both of you!') Realizing that she was in love with him herself, Marie Rambert ran to her cabin to hide her tears.

The circumstances are sufficiently peculiar to make speculation unusually difficult, but it is by no means impossible to believe that Nijinsky's relatively sudden declaration arose from an increasing desire to be free of Diaghilev. Bronia later claimed that their relationship had been under strain for some time, and that Vaslav was only 'himself' when, rarely, parted from his lover. She describes a tremendous row between them which took place at the end of the London season. Diaghilev summoned Bronia to the Savoy, told her that *Jeux* and *Sacre* were disastrously unsuccessful ballets which would never again be performed, that Vaslav could no longer be allowed to experiment in public, and that although he

The Nijinskys at their wedding ceremony; the whole company attended the wedding breakfast.

had promised him that he could choreograph Richard Strauss' *La Légende de Joseph* for the 1914 season, he had now decided to give the ballet to Fokine. He left Bronia to break the news.

Nijinsky was, unsurprisingly, extremely angry – not least because Diaghilev had used Bronia as an intermediary. His bitterness was extreme – and apart from evidently finding their personal relationship intolerable, he accused Diaghilev of destroying his own creation, the Ballets Russes. Diaghilev responded by suggesting to Bronia that Vaslav should leave the company, all his roles being taken over by Fokine. This conflicts with the fact that the two were later together at Baden-Baden, talking with Benois about new projects. And after all, if Nijinsky left the company, where was he to go? Because of the difficulties about his military service, he certainly could not return to St Petersburg and the Maryinsky. Marriage to Romola would solve none of his problems; but if he wished to deliver a blow to Diaghilev's pride, to teach him that he was in control of his own life, marriage would certainly be a shrewd way of doing so.

The *Avon* docked for twenty-four hours at Rio,

where Vaslav and Romola went ashore and bought two wedding rings which the jeweller engraved with their names: 'Vaslav – Romola – 1/9/1913'.

As they sailed on to Buenos Aires, the kindly Bolm (who had once been led to believe that Romola cared for him) tried in an embarrassed fashion to explain that the marriage was not a terribly good idea – she might not realize it, but the – er – friendship between Vaslav and Diaghilev was not – well, it was perhaps – um – more than just a friendship. Vaslav could not really be interested in her . . . Romola thanked him, and said she would rather be unhappy serving Nijinsky's genius than be happy without him.

When the company disembarked at Buenos Aries, Nijinsky moved into a large suite on the first floor; Romola, somewhat to her chagrin, was in a small room on the third. After the first rehearsal at the Teatro Colon, the engaged couple went to the Church of San Miguel, where Nijinsky made his confession to a priest who understood neither Russian nor Polish, and Romola was made to promise to prevent him from dancing in that immoral ballet, *Schéhérazade*. On Wednesday, 10 September, they were married first at a civil ceremony and then at the church, before going straight to the theatre to rehearse *Schéhérazade*, Nijinsky in his usual role, and Romola (for the first time, it seems) as a member of the *corps de ballet*. They then went back to the hotel and had supper, after which Vaslav kissed Romola's hand, and they went to their separate rooms. She locked her door, and piled the furniture against it. It does not seem a specially auspicious start to the marriage.

The Buenos Aires season was a great success. And so, on the surface at least, seemed the marriage, despite initial difficulties. The couple conversed in a mixture of Russian and French; she smoked, he hated smoking; she was never to be more than a com-

Nijinsky and his wife leaving the City Hall, Buenos Aires, on 10 September 1913, after the civil marriage ceremony.

petent dancer, he was a genius. But even if as yet Romola seemed to Marie Rambert not to be in love with her husband, he was evidently very happy, in a continual good humour, sending Romola every day a bunch of roses carried by the glowering Vassili – Diaghilev's valet, accompanying Vaslav purely in order to keep him out of trouble. Eventually, the marriage was consummated. Later, Vaslav confided that he did not regret his relationship with Diaghilev, 'even if morals condemn it,' and very firmly told her that if she ever met anyone she loved more than him, she must let him know; her happiness was paramount to him.

Vaslav had written to Diaghilev with the news of his marriage, naively insisting on his admiration for and devotion to the impresario. Bronia and Liota, on the other hand, read about the marriage in a newspaper. Liota was not pleased.

Diaghilev received the news in Venice. After a brief fit of hysteria, he shut himself up with his emotions, saying nothing to anyone; a member of the company, seeing him sitting alone at a café table and going up to him, saw a face so racked with grief that she was frightened, and backed away. To Vaslav, he sent neither congratulations nor reproaches.

The Buenos Aires season over, there were performances in Montevideo, then in Rio – where Romola discovered that she was pregnant. The company then returned to Europe, and the Nijinskys left the ship at Cadiz to travel on by train to Budapest, where Vaslav would meet Romola's mother, and then to St Petersburg, where Liota was looking after Bronia and her newly-born daughter. But first, to Paris, for a meeting with Diaghilev. Diaghilev was not there. Vaslav cabled him to ask when rehearsals were to start, and when he could begin work on the new ballet. Diaghilev dictated a reply which his *régisseur*, Grigoriev, sent in his own name: LE BALLET RUSSE N'A PLUS BESOIN DE VOS

SERVICES. NE NOUS REJOIGNEZ PAS. When Vaslav questioned this cold dismissal, he was informed that he had broken his contract with the Diaghilev Ballet by refusing to dance a performance of *Le Carnaval* in Rio, and that Diaghilev 'will not therefore require your further services'.

Vaslav never had a formal contract with Diaghilev. More than that, it was actually the case that he had received no salary since the formation of the company in 1911. The agreement was that he should receive 200,000 francs for ten months' work (Karsavina and Fokine received the same amount for six months' work). But during 1911, 1912 and 1913 he had received nothing – though his hotel bills had been paid by Diaghilev, and clothes and ballet shoes had been provided (he needed a new pair of shoes for each performance). And Diaghilev had sent a modest 500 francs to Liota each month.

In Rio – perhaps encouraged by Romola – Vaslav had refused to go on for one performance, as a protest at the non-payment of the back salary Diaghilev owed him; the following day some money was found, and Nijinsky continued to dance as usual. It was fairly clear that the whole of his back salary would now never be paid – and more, Vaslav had lost a second father. Though Romola was to deny it, it seems likely that the trauma of the rejection started the process which was to lead to his eventual total breakdown.

Romola immediately realized the practical significance of the break with Diaghilev, but Nijinsky at first declined to believe the cable. Then he heard that Diaghilev had re-engaged Fokine as *premier danseur* (dancing all Vaslav's roles) and choreographer. Fokine signed a contract on condition that none of Nijinsky's ballets should ever again be performed by Diaghilev's company. Meanwhile, a handsome young dancer from the Bolshoi Theatre was also engaged, and soon became Diaghilev's constant companion: his name was Leonide Massine.

Nijinsky was now faced with a future in which if he wished to continue dancing and to compose new ballets he would have to form his own company – for he could not return to Russia without being liable for military service. Bronia and Liota had made strenuous efforts to have him released from the obligation, even appealing to the War Ministry. The attorney they engaged told them that while he was waiting to see the Minister a woman in expensive furs left his office; and when the interview finally took place, the Minister simply said that Nijinsky's petition had been denied: if he returned to Russia he would have to serve three years in the service. Bronia clearly believed that the Minister's mysterious visitor was Kchessinskaya.

After turning down a number of requests for personal appearances, Vaslav set off for Paris, where the Paris Opéra hoped to negotiate a contract engaging him as choreographer and *premier danseur* at the Opéra at a salary of 100,000 gold francs a year. But he found the repertory there too narrow; he wanted to continue to create new ballets, and soon Bronia and her husband received a cable asking them to join a company he had formed – he had signed a contract with Alfred Butt to dance for eight weeks at the Palace Theatre, London, in the spring of 1914, for one thousand pounds a week. Bronia agreed to become his principal ballerina, and brought from Russia a group of Imperial School graduates – all girls. In London four English girls (who were all provided with Russian names, as was the custom) were engaged: they were to receive twenty-five pounds a week. The company eventually consisted of ten women and two men – Bronia's husband and Nijinsky himself.

Bronia wondered from the first whether the project was not heading for disaster. For one thing, Vaslav planned to present some of Fokine's ballets, and surely that would cause repercussions with that tetchy individual? Apparently, Nijinsky's contracts specified that he should appear in his most famous roles – and he planned to get round the difficulties by re-choreographing the works himself. To that end, he commissioned Ravel to choose and orchestrate a new set of pieces by Chopin from which he would create his own *Sylphides*.

London greeted Nijinsky enthusiastically: Lady Ottoline met him at the Savoy with an enormous bouquet, and the general feeling was that his marriage made him even more acceptable as a society idol. But problems soon began. *Sylphides*, which was to open the season, was prepared very quickly indeed, and with much greater facility than Nijinsky had shown when he was choreographing *Sacre* or *Jeux*. But he was under great strain, and was also disturbed by the fact that the ballets were to be seen in the atmosphere of a music-hall, danced as part of a variety bill and followed by a demonstration of the bioscope. Coping with hairdressers and dressmakers and stage-hands in his vestigial English placed an additional strain on him, and almost the last straw was the ruin of the sets for *L'Après-Midi d'un Faune* by a fire inspector who caused them to be soaked in fireproofing liquid. It was worrying, also, that tickets were not selling well.

Just before the curtain went up on the first performance, on 2 March, Nijinsky received an understandable but mischievous telegram from Pavlova: CONGRATULATIONS BEST WISHES TO MUSIC HALL ARTIST. She was taking her revenge for Vaslav's open disapproval of her, some years previously, for appearing in the self-same theatre on the same kind of variety bill. But instead of smiling wryly, Nijinsky was extremely upset. Then, as he was standing with Bronia in the opening group of *Les Sylphides*, and the curtain went up, they both saw, in a smudge of reflected light from the orchestra pit, the figure of Diaghilev sitting in the front row of the stalls.

Nevertheless, the performance seemed to go well even if they noticed that Diaghilev did not join in the applause. The critics, however, thought that something was missing: Cyril Beaumont, who was in the audience, wrote sadly, 'Nijinsky no longer danced like a god.'

Tension grew worse. There was misunderstanding between Vaslav and Alfred Butt, the theatre's manager, and the audience (which consisted largely of music-hall followers) was alienated when Nijinsky insisted that the lights should be kept lowered during the *entr'actes*, and no music played – there was a lot of restless chatter, and some slow clapping. Then when, at Butt's orders, the orchestra one night struck up a light waltz just before the start of *Spectre*, Vaslav became hysterical, screamed, and refused to dance, though eventually Bronia persuaded him.

During the third week Nijinsky failed to appear. Making an announcement to the audience, Butt explained that the dancer had quite suddenly collapsed with a temperature of 103°. Influenza was suspected, and then confirmed – but the talk was that Nijinsky had had a nervous breakdown. When he had missed three consecutive performances, he was accused of breaching his contract, and the season was cancelled; the costumes, scenery props and music were thrown out of the theatre and sent to a warehouse (they were sold during the war to pay storage debts). The dancers told Vaslav they would be content with their salaries to date and return fare to Russia for those who had come from St Petersburg; but he insisted on paying them a full year's money. It is said that he lost £30,000 on the season. The comedian Fred Emney was engaged as a stop-gap. Nijinsky had danced for the last time in London.

After the two months it took Nijinsky to recover from his illness he and Romola went to Vienna for the birth of their child. Vaslav made an excursion to Madrid to dance (for a fee of three thousand dollars) at a wedding reception given at the American Embassy by the King and Queen of Spain, for Kermit Roosevelt. At the première of Diaghilev's 1914 Paris season, members of the audience stood to watch as he entered the auditorium of the Opéra and made his way to a seat – thoroughly at ease, the gossip writers said – to watch Fokine's new ballet *The Legend of Joseph* danced by Massine. In the interval he made his way to a box where Cocteau and some other friends were sitting; he was greeted by cold silence. He was perhaps cheered by the notices, which were lukewarm: one critic, Jacques Reviere, wrote: 'One must say it boldly: the Russian Ballet was Nijinsky. He alone gave life to the whole company.' Later, Vaslav took a class with Cecchetti – and Diaghilev sent Massine along to watch him work. The new star noticed how quietly Vaslav accepted the old ballet-master's every correction.

On 19 June, in Vienna, Kyra Nijinsky was born. She was late arriving, and a friend sent the Nijinskys tickets for a performance of Richard Strauss' opera *Electra*, on the grounds that if that score did not bring on the baby, nothing would. Next day, Kyra was born. When he heard the child was a girl (he had already decided to call it Vladislav) Vaslav threw his gloves to the floor in momentary irritation; but at the first sight of Kyra, fell in love with her. Meanwhile, friends in London worked busily to try to reconcile Diaghilev and himself; Lady Ripon even blackmailed Diaghilev into re-engaging him, on pain of cancellation of the entire season. Vaslav came to London, but Diaghilev refused to meet him, and Romola reports that Fokine saw to it that the company behaved so coolly to him that one rehearsal was all he could bear. In fact, as Richard Buckle suggests, he may simply have realised that under the terms of Fokine's contract with Diaghilev, he, Nijinsky, could never be permitted to dance with the company. He returned to Vienna.

By now the shadow of the First World War was falling over Europe after the assassination at Sarajevo. Lady Ripon tried to persuade the Nijinskys to come to London, but Romola was unwell and they decided to stay in Vienna until the end of the summer and then make for Russia via Budapest. But when they tried to leave Budapest they found the Russian border closed and they were arrested as enemy subjects and detained under house arrest (and in the house of Romola's unfriendly family) as prisoners of war.

Ironically, Diaghilev was by now desperate to engage Vaslav again, both as dancer and choreographer; but for the first time ever Vaslav spent a whole year without dancing – there was simply nowhere for him to practise – though not without thinking of the ballet, and of the possibility of choreographing Richard Strauss' tone-poem *Till Eulenspiegel*.

Romola's mother found it deeply embarrassing that she, 'the first actress of Hungary', should have a Russian son-in-law – and Vaslav still felt Russian: when asked to dance in aid of injured Hungarian troops, he refused unless half the proceeds were given for the care of Russian prisoners-of-war; the condition was not accepted. Madame de Pulszky continually tried to persuade her daughter to divorce Vaslav at the earliest opportunity – not only, after all, was he a Russian, but an out-of-work Russian.

He and Romola alleviated their boredom by reading together – Chekhov, Tolstoy, Pushkin. Vaslav helped care for Kyra and made her delightful wooden toys. But the tension was fearful: at one stage Romola actually pleaded with the authorities to send the three of them to a prison camp in preference to their remaining at home. The favour was refused. Meanwhile, her mother informed the police

Nijinsky with the score of Till Eulenspiegel; *Richard Strauss was so impressed by his conception that he offered to alter the score if the choreographer required it.*

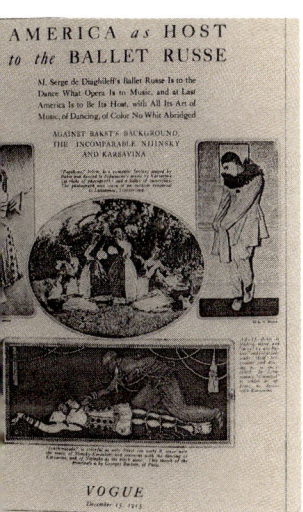

The Ballets Russes' visit to America in 1916 was heralded by all sorts of press stories, some more knowledgeable than others.

that Vaslav was making notes in code about military installations. Fortunately, Vaslav managed to convince the chief of police that his strange hieroglyphics were in fact a newly-invented form of dance notation. Shortly afterwards, they were informed that they were to be transferred to Carlsbad in Bohemia; but the chief of police suggested that they should break their journey in Vienna – he was obviously hinting that they should use the opportunity to escape.

Diaghilev had by now assured his American contacts that Nijinsky would be dancing for his company during its coming tour of the U.S., and a group of distinguished men and women were agitating for the dancer's release: Lady Ripon, Queen Alexandra, the Dowager Empress Marie Feodorovna, the Emperor Franz-Joseph, the King of Spain – even the Pope. Gradually the situation eased. In Vienna, Vaslav was given permission to practise on the stage of the Theater an der Wien, and worked on his choreography for the Liszt *Mephisto Waltz*, for a Japanese ballet, and for *Till Eulenspiegel* – Richard Strauss came to see him, and was delighted at his ideas for the ballet, even offering to amend the score if need be.

The Ballets Russes gave its first performance in New York on 12 January 1916. A short two-week season at the small Century Theatre on Central Park West was greeted rather coolly by the critics: Massine and Bolm, Lopokhova and Tchernicheva were fine, but where were the real stars? Where were Karsavina and Pavlova? Above all, where was Nijinsky? His absence was certainly noted; but his work was plainly to be seen – particularly *L'Après-Midi d'un Faune*, in which the Faun was danced by Massine, and which was seen all too clearly. The ending, the *New York American* said, was 'daringly suggestive,' while the *New York Tribune* decided not to summarise the story of the ballet, since 'we do not intend to risk prosecution'. After complaints to the Police Department by members of the Catholic Theatre Movement, the final movements of the ballet were adjusted – instead of lying on the scarf, Massine merely sat and looked at it. When Nijinsky arrived, his sheer artistry was somewhat to defuse the situation – though Carl van Vechten was to write that as the Slave in *Schéhérazade* his appearance and movements were so redolent of exotic eroticism that 'its very existence seems incredible on our puritanic stage'.

Back in Vienna, on 1 February, Vaslav was summoned to the American Embassy and told that he could leave for America provided Romola and Kyra remained in Vienna as hostages. He refused, and eventually all three were given permission to leave. There was considerable publicity when it was announced that Nijinsky would dance at the Metropolitan Opera House in April; Romola's mother appeared in Vienna to congratulate her distinguished and famous son-in-law. When she approached him, he simply looked at her and asked: 'Who is this lady?' It was the only time Romola saw him act so coldly to anyone.

Issued with an elaborate Russian diplomatic passport, the family crossed to America on an elderly French liner, the *Rochambeau*, and arrived in New York on 4 April. Diaghilev met the ship, pressed a bouquet on Romola, kissed Vaslav on both cheeks and unenthusiastically, but with an eye to the press cameras, took Kyra in his arms. They all left the quay together.

But Nijinsky had won a court order in London for money Diaghilev still owed him for past performances, and now declined to dance until the debt was paid. As the *New York Times* put it in a headline: NOT A TOE WILL EX-WAR PRISONER TWINKLE TILL ANTE IS RAISED. Eventually, Diaghilev promised to pay the debt by instalments, and Vaslav appeared for the first time in New York on 12 April in *Spectre* and *Petrushka*, going on to dance *Carnaval, Les Sylphides, Narcisse* and *Schéhérazade*. The general impression is that some members of the company who had been familiar with his dancing in the past felt that it had deteriorated; those who had not seen him before were impressed. Massine, for instance, found every moment, every gesture, remarkable: 'After seeing Nijinsky dance. I realized I had seen a genius,' he remarked in his autobiography.

The critics were somewhat divided: many of them marvelled at his technique and the spirit of his characterisations. His appearance as the Slave in *Schéhérazade* was unpopular with racists, who caused trouble throughout the tour, especially in the south. One critic wrote that, 'the impulse to jump on the stage and thrash [the Slave] must be suppressed,' while it was seriously suggested that 'black' and 'white' characters should not appear on stage at the same time. *Narcisse*, never very successful, was almost a disaster. One newspaper headline summarised:

NIJINSKY DANCES: AUDIENCE LAUGHS ... MYTHOLOGICAL POEM EFFEMINATE EXHIBIT. STORY OF NARCISSUS AND THE SPRING, TOLD TERPSICHOREAN FASHION, GREETED BY GIGGLES.

Spectre might have had the same kind of reception, but though *Musical America* spoke of 'a most unprepossessing effeminacy', the ballet received a ten-minute ovation, and other critics were admiring.

In an interview at the time, Nijinsky had a word to say about his characterization in *Narcisse* and other roles:

One must be [he said] as a changing chameleon in the varying roles one enacts ... One must be prepared with shades to enhance one's meaning – in the morning, perhaps a boy, at noon a creature sans sex, at night a fullgrown man... For instance in *Narcisse*, there is no virility, only boyish pureness. Effeminate it is not – for even in adolescence a boy is not like a girl. True, he is not yet a man, any more than she is a woman, but there the resemblance ends. His thoughts and desires are different, therefore his movements are different.

Relationships with Diaghilev were far from calm: according to Romola, he lost no opportunity of blackguarding Vaslav to the press, or spreading rumours about his prima-donna-like behaviour. Nevertheless it was not an unhappy time. Vaslav loved the bustle of New York, and spent hours wandering along Broadway simply watching the passing show. He discovered Coca-Cola; one glass of it was, however, enough. He discovered 'the movies', too – alas, they never discovered him; it is astonishing that not a single frame of film of him seems ever to have been taken, even at the Chaplin studios when he visited them later, and met 'Charlie', who he so much admired.

New York society took him to its heart: he and Romola were invited to stay for weekends at many of the most opulent houses on Long Island ('*Très Ballets Russes!*' Vaslav would comment on the beautifully decorated bathrooms). He bought a Peerless *coupé* and proudly drove Romola and Kyra about; he was an excellent driver on the straight, but had no idea how to turn corners, and blithely disregarded every rule of the road. On hills, he would try every gear in turn, and if none appeared to work, would allow the car to run backwards to the bottom. He and Romola were often seen with the great tenor Enrico Caruso and the violinist Fritz Kreisler, and when they appeared at restaurants a spotlight would be trained on their table while their presence was announced to other diners. One evening they dined with Isadora Duncan, and there was an embarrassed silence when Isadora reminded Vaslav that she had once asked him to father her child: 'I see you have changed now,' she said; 'you are less intolerant towards us women.'

There were parties and special appearances – at, for instance, an evening of *tableaux vivants* in aid of a fund to help the people of Venice, where there had recently been a disastrous flood. Vaslav appeared as a Carpaccio gondolier; while he was on stage, some of the society women who had paid two hundred and fifty dollars to attend went to his dressing-room and stole his underclothes.

Otto Khan, the American impresario, was eager to arrange a coast-to-coast tour of the States for 1917, but felt – with some justice – that the strained relationship between Nijinsky and Diaghilev would hardly contribute to its success. He easily persuaded Vaslav that he should be his own artistic director for such a tour and that Diaghilev's presence was unnecessary. Diaghilev was forced, for economic reasons, to agree; while he accompanied the company back to Europe to appear in Madrid, the Nijinskys remained in New York, and Vaslav began to make plans for the production of *Till Eulenspiegel*.

The prospect of heavy responsibility ahead seems to have weighed on his mind. Robert Edmund Jones, the young designer engaged for *Till*, noticed how the flesh at the side of Vaslav's thumbs had been bitten until it bled, and got: 'the impression of something too eager, too brilliant, a quivering of the nerves, a nature racked to dislocation by a merciless creative urge'.

When the company met once more in New York early in September, there were only three weeks in which to prepare *Till*. It was a very difficult time. Romola was convinced that Diaghilev had ordered the dancers not to co-operate with Vaslav; she also believed that he ordered the conductor, Pierre Monteux, not to appear with the company (in fact,

Nijinsky in rehearsal dress, in New York in 1916, when it seems he was on the edge of mental breakdown.

his refusal to conduct *Till* was a gesture against its composer, who had signed an Austrian manifesto against Monteux's native France). The dancers, meanwhile, thought that Nijinsky was behaving very strangely. Rehearsals went so badly that the *corps* at one point went on strike. Sokolova recalled that: 'at the beginning, Nijinsky turned up quite normally, and would wander about and arrange a little bit of a dance here and a little bit of a dance there ... but after about two weeks of this we saw that nothing was progressing whatsoever'. Then he simply declined to appear at rehearsals, and when he was brought to the theatre he fell and sprained his ankle and was ordered to rest.

At the dress rehearsal, Sokolova said, 'we did

the little bits we knew, we saw the costumes, which were very beautiful, and the decor; we did as much as there was to do, and then we just stood – because there was no more'. Nijinsky returned to his hotel and locked himself in his room. The theatre was sold out for two performances of the ballet.

At the first night, Sokolova remembered, they danced what they knew, and then improvised, while Nijinsky himself seemed to invent his role as he went along. Nevertheless, the evening was a triumph; Monteux applauded from a stage box; Pavlova from a stall. There were fifteen curtain calls, and many of the critics were ecstatic: '. . . a brilliant performance . . .'; '. . . a triumph of stagecraft and choreography . . .'; '. . . a complete success . . .'; 'Nijinsky's masterpiece . . .'. If the ballet was as unprepared as Sokolova suggested, its reception is an enormous tribute to Nijinsky's powers of creative improvisation, though Robert Jones' designs were evidently very beautiful, and contributed much to its success. Nijinsky himself thought that *Till* was: 'produced too quickly. It was "taken out of the oven" too soon, and therefore was raw. The American public liked my "raw" ballet. It tasted good, as I cooked it very well . . . I made it a comic ballet, as everyone was fed up with the war. People had to be cheered up. I cheered them up.' Indeed, while preparing the ballet, he could be heard constantly repeating to himself, '*Pour faire rire, pour faire rire*,' and Robert Jones said that everything about the piece was irresistibly comic.

Diaghilev, of course, was not present; he never saw the ballet. The following night, Nijinsky danced *L'Après-Midi d'un Faune* for the first time in America: 'there was nothing in his acting to bring a blush of shame to the cheek of modesty,' said one critic.

After New York the company started on its five-month tour: sixty-five dancers, sixty musicians, technicians, scenery, costumes, props in a twelve-

Nijinsky making up one of the dancers in his last ballet, Till Eulenspiegel *(1916)*

carriage special train travelled from city to city right across the country – Providence, New Haven, Brooklyn, Springfield, Boston, Worcester, Hartford, Bridgeport, Atlantic City, Baltimore, Washington, Philadelphia, Columbia, New Orleans (where Romola insisted on visiting one of the famous brothels, and Vaslav, accompanying her, chatted to the whores and bought them drinks), Houston, Austin, Fort Worth, Dallas, Tulsa, Wichita, Kansas City and finally to the West Coast, where the company visited the Chaplin studios.

There were some pleasant times – socialising, visits to football games and swimming galas, meetings with artists and musicians and even politicians – in Washington Vaslav was able to thank President Wilson personally for his help in releasing the family from imprisonment in Austria.

But during the tour, Vaslav became increasingly distraught. Things got off to a bad start when, while the company was in Boston, the *New York Times* printed a rumour that he had been ordered by the Russian War Office to return to his country to report for military service 'on penalty of being considered a deserter'. When they arrived at Atlanta they were greeted with a demand that Vaslav should report to the military authorities in St Petersburg in ten days' time. The whole thing was, of course, a nonsense. Sokolova, dancing major roles with him, found life very difficult indeed. 'He would sometimes lock himself in his dressing-room and say, "No, I'm not going to dance *Sylphides*, I'm going to dance *Carnaval*",' she remembered. 'Well, the décor for *Carnaval* just wasn't there, it had gone on somewhere else; so they used to take the costume for *Sylphides* into his dressing-room and lock him in, and he'd put on the *Sylphides* costume and come out and dance the programme just as though nothing had been said or done.'

During the tour, he taught her *Spectre de la*

Nijinsky as Till Eulenspiegel, a figure all gaiety and wit, in retrospect a moving contrast to his off-stage personality, now increasingly tense and difficult.

Rose. But, 'it was one of the most terrifying things I've ever done on stage, because when he went to hold out his arm for me to rest my hand on his shoulder and take an arabesque, he would just slide it away and leave me suspended, unprotected; and then in the lifts he just threw you in the air and you were lucky if you were caught properly when you came down.'

There was also the odd matter of the Tolstoyans. A Polish dancer called Dmitri Kostrovsky had attached himself to Nijinsky like a leech, from the moment rehearsals for *Till* had begun in New York. Romola reported how 'he followed Vaslav everywhere like a dog, eagerly looking for a smile'. She noticed that he was given to collecting little groups of dancers around him, talking earnestly to – or at – them. It was explained to her that Kostrovsky was a disciple of Tolstoy, convinced that the great writer's theories could save the world; he was trying to convert everyone.

Nijinsky was easy game. Kostrovsky and his colleague and follower Nicolas Zverev would even come to Vaslav's sleeping-coach during the tour and talk to him in Russian, which Romola could not understand. Soon, Vaslav was seen to be wearing simple Russian peasant shirts, and became increasingly introspective and gloomy. He became a vegan and increasingly seemed to have less stamina. Romola learned that he was now planning to give up dancing and become a farm worker. Deciding that only a shock would shake him out of all this, she threatened to leave him, and for the last six weeks of the tour returned to New York while the company went on through Michigan, Ohio, Indiana and Tennessee. The press reports of the tour (collected in Nesta Macdonald's *Diaghilev Observed*) reflect a very American reception from ordinary theatregoers and critics unused to the ballet. A San Francisco newspaper described Nijinsky as, 'an All-

American half-back – gone wrong,' and at St Paul, when poor attendances forced price reductions, the newspaper headline was 'LEGS PRICE COMING DOWN'!

When Vaslav rejoined Romola in New York for the last performances of the season – towards the end of February, 1917 – she noticed with relief that he was once more wearing collars and ties, and his rings had reappeared on his fingers. But now there was some difficulty about future plans. Diaghilev had telegrammed an invitation to Vaslav to join the company in Spain, and later on a tour of South America. Vaslav was not enthusiastic, but certainly it was not possible to remain in America, for the conditions of Vaslav's release from Austria included a clause that he could not dance in any country that was not neutral – and it was obvious that America was about to enter the war. Italy was an Allied country, so he could not go with the company to appear there. Russia was impossible. A telegram was sent to Diaghilev: 'EN PRINCIPE J'ACCEPTE DISCUTERONS PROJECTS EN ESPAGNE.' Diaghilev was delighted; he knew, as the Nijinskys did not, that at that time a cable was accepted as a binding contract.

The Nijinskys sailed back to Europe on a Spanish ship which had for some time been wrecked, and was only recently recovered from the sea-bed. There were so many rats in the cabins that despite the cold Romola slept on deck throughout the voyage. They landed in Cadiz and made their way to Madrid, where they made their home at the Ritz, and Vaslav practised at the Royal Theatre, which the King placed at his disposal. He was still working on his system of ballet notation, and beginning to think of preparing a ballet to one of the poems of the Indian writer Rabindranath Tagore. He also became fascinated by Spanish dancing, and persuaded some gypsy dancers to teach him Flamenco.

They spent a month or two in Madrid before

Diaghilev appeared, to greet Vaslav as enthusiastically as though there had never been any breach between them. Diaghilev was very excited by the choreography of young Massine – *Les Femmes de Bonne Humeur*, to Scarlatti's music, for instance – and was eager for Vaslav's opinion. He also spoke enthusiastically about the South American tour; he introduced the Nijinskys to Picasso, who was working with Massine on designs for *Parade*; and he was eager – he said – for a new ballet from Nijinsky.

'You see,' said Vaslav to Romola; 'I always told you he was my friend.'

Vaslav got on well with Massine. The latter admired the way in which Nijinsky immediately grasped what he was trying to do in his new ballets, and was touched when the older dancer volunteered to appear in *The Good-Humoured Ladies* if that would help to publicize it. When rehearsals started of Vaslav's own work, Massine was full of admiration for the consummate way in which his colleague was able to demonstrate precisely the effect he required in *L'Après-Midi d'un Faune*.

The company gave a few performances in Madrid – the King and Queen came almost every night to see Nijinsky dance his old roles in *Schéhérazade*, *Carnaval*, *Le Spectre* and *L'Après-Midi d'un Faune*. King Alfonso was much impressed, and in private attempted to reproduce Vaslav's leaps; not, it seems, with any remarkable success. There were then some performances in Barcelona.

All seemed to be well; yet Romola was uneasy. Whatever her motives in marrying him, and whatever the basic truth about their relationship, it is clear that she now loved her husband; and she feared that Diaghilev wanted to recapture him. There was trouble, again, with the Tolstoyans: Kostrovsky and Zverev had once more insinuated themselves into Vaslav's life, and Romola was quite sure that Diaghilev was behind that, too – that he realized that by playing on

Vaslav's deeply religious sense he could alienate him from his wife and regain the ascendancy. Vaslav showed a little resistance this time, however; when Kostrovsky rebuked him for eating meat, he at least replied that he needed the strength for his performances ('Then give up dancing,' was Kostrovsky's reply!). But they were particularly clever at insinuating ideas which they knew would appeal to Vaslav, and when he suggested to Romola that perhaps sexual relationships between a man and a woman, even within marriage, were only permissible with the object of procreation, she decided that at all costs he must be prevented from going to South America with the company, where the Tolstoyans could finally wean him away from her.

But though she managed to persuade Vaslav to turn down the tour, Diaghilev insisted that his contract required it. Vaslav pointed out that he had no contract. Diaghilev replied that the cable Vaslav had sent from America constituted a binding contract. Vaslav left the luncheon-table (it was the last meal he and Diaghilev were to share), and that afternoon he and Romola decided to leave the company. As they were boarding the train for Madrid, they were arrested by the Civil Guard. The arrest proved to be illegal; but Nijinsky's cable to Diaghilev also proved to be a legal contract. Lawyers engaged by Romola, however, drew up a much tighter one, which among other things agreed that Nijinsky should be paid his full fee in gold an hour before every performance. Diaghilev grudgingly signed it.

Diaghilev saw Vaslav dance for the last time at the Teatro Liceo, Barcelona, on 30 June 1917; shortly afterwards the Nijinskys sailed for South America in the *Reina Victoria Eugenia*. Vaslav was exhausted, though he did learn the tango from a young Chilean on the boat – a man who was later to marry an heiress and, as the Marquis de Cuevas, to found his own ballet company.

Diaghilev – charming, inflexible, protective, infuriating; art was his religion, and humans were subservient to it.

The tour started well for Romola. Kostrovsky had been behaving more oddly than ever, and occasionally fell to the ground in a fit. His wife persuaded him to consult a specialist in Montevideo, and he was pronounced incurably insane and dispatched back to Russia. But even with the Tolstoyans no longer so dangerous, the tour was fearfully unhappy. The company treated Vaslav, or seemed to treat him, as a leper; Grigoriev, its manager, was totally loyal to Diaghilev, and thought of Romola, in particular, as an enemy (the sight of her sitting in Vaslav's dressing-room before each performance, watch in hand, waiting for Grigoriev to hand over his fee in gold coins, must indeed have been irrritating). Then came a series of unfortunate accidents: Vaslav stepped on a rusty nail; a heavy weight fell from the flies and almost hit him; one night the whole structure of the magician's stall in *Petrushka* began to collapse with him on top of it. Could someone be trying to injure or even kill him? Both Romola and Vaslav appear to have suffered from a massive persecution complex; yet certainly some very strange incidents seem to have occurred. She employed detectives to watch over him, after which – she says – the accidents miraculously ceased.

Audiences, however, applauded his dancing as whole-heartedly as ever, and people who met him socially – including various ambassadors – found his behaviour charming and entirely rational. The French Ambassador in Rio was the poet Paul Claudel, who had on his staff the composer Darius Milhaud: they had planned two ballets together – one of which was later produced as *Le Création du Monde* – while Milhaud was to compose the score of *Le Train Bleu* for Diaghilev and his last young *protegée*, Anton Dolin. Both men disliked the old-fashioned *Sylphides*, but entirely appreciated Nijinsky's genius as a dancer – Claudel praised his every movement, as natural as those of an animal, his enormous authority on stage, the way in which even in repose he still seemed to be composing his movements and his poses; Milhaud remembered his supreme muscular control, even in a simple gesture such as turning his head to speak to someone behind him.

Vaslav does not seem to have allowed the rigours of the tour to distress him unduly. The composer Estrade Guerra, who met him in Rio, found him highly strung, but not abnormally so. He was astonished, later, to hear of Vaslav's insanity: 'Nothing in our meetings in Brazil could have led me to foresee that.'

On 26 September 1917, Nijinsky danced *Le Spectre de la Rose* in Buenos Aires. It was his last appearance with the Diaghilev Ballet. He danced once more in Montevideo, at a gala which he had organised in aid of the French and English Red Cross. He had choreographed some new dances for the programme, which he danced to the music of Chopin, dressed in his *Sylphides* costume and the pink shoes he wore in *Spectre*. At the end of his appearance, he made two enormous jumps which took him right across the stage and a third, at the apogee of which, as at his first Paris appearance years before – he vanished from sight. He was never to be seen again on a public stage.

Nijinsky was twenty-nine. He had always intended to dance until he was in his mid-thirties, then to retire and start a school of dance and choreography in which 'the balance and co-ordination of musical, scenic and choreographic elements' would be taught, and a modern dancer produced who would be 'a thorough musician and an actor . . . with a knowledge of painting and the principles of pictorial art'. In other words, a Diaghilev dancer.

In Lausanne the Nijinskys were reunited with Kyra and took a house, the Villa Guardamunt, in the mountains above St Moritz. There they spent a quiet

The Russian painter Leon Bakst (1866–1924) was a close friend of Diaghilev and one of the founders of the Ballets Russes; he designed a dozen ballets for the company, and his original use of colour made an enormous impact in fashion and interior decoration, as well as in the theatre.

winter, Vaslav for the first time happy in a home of his own, practising each morning on a ground-floor balcony while Kyra watched, playing with her and with the village children, tobogganing, watching Romola skate, thinking about new ballets – one of them to Debussy's *Chanson de Bilitis*. He also devised a ballet which would show an ideal life: a youth searching for, and finding, the perfect mate. He not only composed the choreography, but also designed the sets – it is at this time that he seems to have begun to draw, seriously, and from the first was fascinated by the form of the perfect circle, and the way in which figures and scenes could be represented by using it.

In the autumn of 1918 he learned in a letter from Bronia of the death of his brother Stanislas. Romola found herself in tears. Vaslav looked at her quietly, and said: 'Do not cry; he was insane; it is better like this.'

The war ended. Diaghilev, Massine and Osbert and Sacheverell Sitwell watched the crowds dancing in Trafalgar Square. In Switzerland Nijinsky had been reading Nietzsche and Maeterlinck and planning a ballet set in a brothel, with the old procuress instructing her girls in the arts of love and life; the part of the old woman was to be a mime role for the great actress Réjane.

But there were to be no more Nijinsky ballets. The dancer was becoming more and more introverted, spending hours pondering religious and ethical questions, working on dance notation, drawing and painting. As part of her attempts to raise money, between the wars, Romola was later to organize exhibitions of his art works; but they are in fact the simple drawings of an emotionally afflicted man, interesting perhaps as psychological evidence, but otherwise (as one critic has put it) merely 'charts of the closing down of his mind'.

One day, as Romola was dressing Kyra for a

walk, he suddenly came out of his room and violently upbraided her for making too much noise:

I looked up, surprised. His face, his manner were strange; he had never spoken to me like this. 'I am sorry. I did not realise we were so loud.' Vaslav got hold of me then by my shoulders and shook me violently. I clasped Kyra in my arms very close, then with one powerful movement Vaslav pushed me down the stairs. I lost my balance and fell with the child, who began to scream. I stood up, more astounded than terrified . . . I turned round, exclaiming, 'You ought to be ashamed! You are behaving like a *moujik!*' A very changed Vaslav we found when we came home, docile and kind as ever. I did not speak about the incident, either to him or anyone else.

A few days later Nijinsky was found wandering the streets wearing a gold cross, stopping pedestrians and urging them to go to church. Romola was forced to consult a doctor, who diagnosed mild hysteria, but advised a male nurse, who was introduced into the house in the guise of a masseur. Vaslav was not deceived, but accepted the situation. A few weeks later, he calmly announced to some friends that, missing the stage, he had decided to play the part of a lunatic – and had done so to such effect that Romola had been deceived, and had engaged a male nurse to look after him. It was all a great joke.

In January, 1919, he decided to give a dance recital for some Viennese friends, in aid of the Red Cross. He refused to tell Romola what he would dance; refused even to tell the pianist who was to accompany him. When his wife asked what the pianist should prepare, he answered: 'I will tell her at the time. Do not speak. *Silence!* This is my marriage with God!'

Descriptions of the embarrassing evening which followed vary, but it is clear that, before an audience of about two hundred, he first presented a mime (to Chopin's Prelude No. 20 in C minor), then danced a piece with many of his old acrobatic leaps. Then he stopped, put his hands over his heart, and said, 'The little horse is tired.'

Finally, according to Romola, he took some rolls of black and white velvet and laid them out in the form of a cross on the floor:

> He stood at the head of it with open arms, a living cross himself. "Now I will dance you the war, with its suffering, with its destruction, with its death. The war which you did not prevent and so you are also responsible for." He seemed to fill the room with horror-struck humanity. It was tragic; his gestures were all monumental, and he entranced us so that we almost saw him floating over corpses... We felt that Vaslav was like one of those overpowering creatures full of dominating strength: a tiger let out from the jungle, who in any moment could destroy us. And he was dancing, dancing on... It was the dance for life against death.

A little later, Romola took Vaslav to Zurich, where the psychiatrist Professor Bleuler talked to him, then made an excuse to see Romola alone. She must take Kyra away, he told her; she must get a divorce. Vaslav was incurably insane.

For the next thirty years and more, Romola Nijinsky led the life of a heroine. She did not for one moment consider deserting her husband, and only for the most pressing reasons left him even for a few hours. Bleuler had diagnosed his condition as schizophrenia – a term he had invented. When Romola's mother and step-father arrived in Zurich, she was unwise enough to tell them. They attempted, unsuccessfully, to persuade her to a divorce; then while her mother took her for a walk, Pardany summoned a police ambulance which carried Vaslav off to the state asylum, where he was found by Professor Bleuler. The shock of his abduction brought on his first catatonic attack.

Bleuler advised Romola to take Nijinsky to a sanatorium at Kreuzlingen. He remained there for six months, but at the end of that time had become

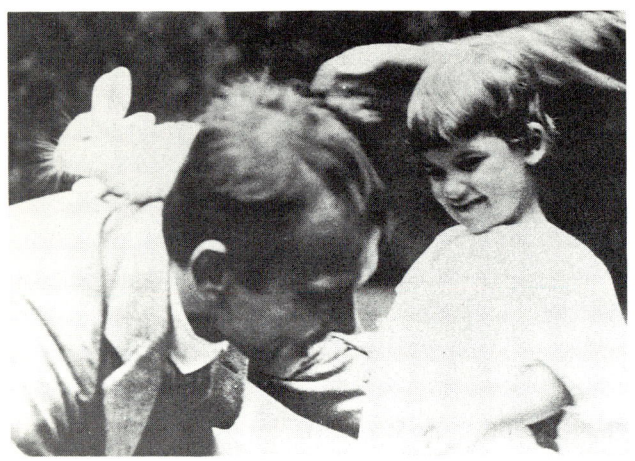

Nijinsky as father: with his daughter Kyra and a pet rabbit.

violent, declining nourishment and continually subject to hallucinations. Romola took him home, then to Vienna, where she cared for him herself, only appealing for help when he became too violent for her to handle. On the one occasion she left the country, she unwisely entrusted him to her parents in Budapest. They committed Vaslav once more to the state asylum. Romola hurried back and removed him to Austria. In 1920, she gave birth to their second daughter, Tamara.

Vaslav was by now incapable of work or even of recreation; he knew Romola, but when Liota and Bronia came to Vienna in 1921 from Kiev, where she was now running a school, Vaslav recognized neither his mother nor his sister.

Diaghilev heard the news of Nijinsky's madness in London, and Marie Rambert was horrified, taking tea with him and Massine at the Ritz, to hear him describe his former lover as now 'walking on all fours'. But as Richard Buckle points out, Diaghilev was not given to showing his emotion in public; cool irony was more his line.

In 1923 Diaghilev came to see Vaslav for the first time for six years. With an attempt at cheerfulness, he told him he must come once more to dance for the Diaghilev ballet. Nijinsky shook his head: 'I cannot,' he said, 'because I am mad.' The following year, at rehearsals for *Le Train Bleu*, Vaslav watched as Dolin, Diaghilev's new English star, learned from Bronia the marvellously acrobatic choreography with which he was to score a triumph. But he only stared blankly, and eventually Romola led him away.

She never for a moment seems to have given up hope of a cure. She tried everything: she took Vaslav to Lourdes, to Christian Science lectures, to various doctors. And she took him to the ballet – to the Paris Opéra, in 1928, to see Karsavina dance once more in their old ballet *Petrushka*. Serge Lifar, the spectacularly handsome young dancer now working for Diaghilev, came with the impresario to fetch the Nijinskys from their flat. Lifar kissed Nijinsky's hand. Vaslav looked at him for a moment with the fierce gaze of a wild animal; then, 'a wonderful smile lit up his face', Lifar recalled; 'a smile so kindly, so childishly pure, so luminous and undimmed, that I fell utterly under its charm'.

That night, having allowed Lifar to shave him, Nijinsky sat in a box with Diaghilev. Various old friends came to greet him, but he did not recognize them. In the interval before *Petrushka* he was led onto the stage. Karsavina, in her Doll's costume, came up to him. For a moment, she thought he recognized her. She called him by his pet name: Vatza. He turned his head away. A photographer assembled them into a small group. For a moment Nijinsky leaned forward and looked into Karsavina's face; but again dropped his eyes and turned away.

Count Harry Kessler, a German patron of the theatre, was present that evening, and saw Diaghilev with 'a short, haggard youngster wearing a tattered coat'. Looking closer he saw that it was Nijinsky, 'his face, so often radiant as a young god's, for thousands an imperishable memory, now grey, hanging slackly and void of expression, only fleetingly lit by a vacuous smile ... his great eyes were mindless but infinitely touching, like those of a sick animal'.

By now Diaghilev himself was a sick man. After his company's London season, he went with his latest prodigy, the sixteen-year-old composer Igor Markevitch, to Munich to hear *Tristan*, and then on alone to Venice. He had been neglecting the diabetes from which he suffered; he fell ill; and on 19 August 1929, in a room of the Grand Hotel des Bains de Mer – where he had stayed with Nijinsky after that first Paris season of 1909 – he died. Diaghilev's Ballets Russes died with him.

Desperate for money, Romola was forced to work in the United States, and reluctantly placed her husband in the Kreuzlingen Sanatorium, where at least she knew he would be well cared for. In 1936, Kyra Nijinsky married Igor Markevitch, and in the same year Romola edited and published an edition of Vaslav's Diary. Clearly the product of a schizophrenic, it is nevertheless of considerable interest, and in some ways looks forward to many attitudes of the 1980s in its dislike of drugs, its plea for vegetarianism and self-denial, its concern for the poor. Its ramblings sometimes approach a strange poetry:

It was only very occasionally, after 1917, that Nijinsky in any way recalled his years of dancing. A photographer on one occasion, in 1945, caught him in what was only a shadow of one of his legendary leaps.

I am the bull, the wounded bull. I am God in the bull. I am Apis. I am an Egyptian, I am an Indian, I am a Red Indian. I am a Negro. I am a Chinaman. I am a Japanese. I am a foreigner, a stranger. I am a sea bird. I am a land bird. I am the tree of Tolstoy. I am the roots of Tolstoy – Tolstoy is mine. I am his ...

In 1937 Anton Dolin organized a charity matinée in London to raise money to help the Nijinskys. Lifar, Margot Fonteyn, Dolin and Sokolova took part, and £2,500 was raised. The same year Romola mounted her exhibition in London of Nijinsky's drawings, water-colours and pastels – works which, Sir Herbert Read wrote, 'suggest the fully conscious art of Nijinsky – his ballets. The rhythm is a dancing rhythm.'

Among Romola's attempts to make money – which included a lecture tour in the US – she wrote with some help a biography of Nijinsky, which was published in 1933. Among the many fruitless attempts to cast a film about Nijinsky's life was one by Alexander Korda; the script would have been based on Romola's book, and the part of Nijinsky would have been played by the young John Gielgud.

In 1938 Nijinsky underwent a course of insulin shock treatment suggested by Dr Bleuler, long retired but still interested in his case. For a while there was an improvement, and startling rumours started to circulate – Nijinsky was about to dance again, in London, in Paris, in New York . . . When Lifar visited him, Vaslav actually corrected some of the movements the younger dancer made while rehearsing *L'Après-Midi*, and even, suddenly, did one of his old, unprepared spectacular jumps. But it was simply a flash of summer lightning, for though there was some improvement – the hallucinations from which he had suffered ceased – he was still quite capable of turning on Romola. On one occasion he almost pushed her over a cliff, and later threw a tray of food and drink at her.

When the Second World War broke out, Switzerland mobilized, and the attendant who had helped Romola care for Vaslav was called up. A series of nurses were terrified out of their lives by his antagonism; he began more and more to depend on Romola, and though doctors advised her to place him in an asylum, for a while she cared for him without assistance, even managing to cope with the dangerous moments when he threatened to attack her.

She wanted to move to America, but funds from England were cut off by wartime currency regulations, and the Swiss refused her a visa. Though she could have gone to America alone, she decided instead to take Vaslav to Hungary, a neutral country.

No one was at Budapest station to meet them. They went to the Ritz, and Romola telephoned her mother's house, to be told that her parents had left town.

Within a day or two they returned and reluctantly agreed to provide sanctuary. The Nijinskys found themselves in the same rooms they had occupied during the First World War, and putting up with the same antagonism. More than once they were asked to leave, but Romola steadfastly refused: the house had been bought with her father's money, and she believed she was entitled to live there.

There were occasional holidays from what must have been a hideously uncomfortable atmosphere: to a cottage by a lake in the country, for instance, where Vaslav enjoyed the swimming he had always loved.

In March, 1941, the Germans occupied Budapest. Romola feared for Vaslav's life: she knew the treatment the Nazis recommended for the insane – death. When in December, 1941, Hungary declared war on Great Britain and America, she and Vaslav left her parents' home and took a small house on a hill just outside the city. She made a little money by selling copies of Vaslav's Diary from door to door. Later, the kindness of the general manager of the National Bank of Hungary, a ballet fan, provided enough money for them to exist on. They moved to a small border town called Sopron, on the shores of Lake Neusiedler; there was a small hospital there where Romola was able to leave Vaslav when she went briefly back to Budapest to sell some jewellery; on the return journey she saw, from the train, long lines of trucks from which an occasional arm stretched out in appeal. They were laden with Jews being taken to their deaths at the concentration camp at Auschwitz.

Towards the end of the war, with the Russians advancing towards Hungary, the house in which they lived was almost demolished by a bomb; miraculously, Nijinsky was found covered in dust but alive, in a roofless room. Once more, he had to be placed in the hospital. One evening, there was a knock on Romola's door: an attendant from the hospital stood outside, with Vaslav in an old coat carrying a bundle containing his few belongings. The hospital had received instructions to exterminate its mental patients. The attendant had smuggled Vaslav out.

After hiding for some days in caves in a hillside, living off dry biscuits and water while the Germans fled before the advancing Russian troops, the Nijinskys saw the Red Army troops moving west. They walked back to the town. Russian soldiers approached them. 'Nazis!' they shouted, pointing their guns. 'Keep quiet!' Vaslav shouted back – in Russian.

The worst of their troubles were over. Next morning the Russian Commanding Officer summoned Romola, and listened to her account of their life during the war. Then he gave her official identification papers. Friendly Russian soldiers called on them, and Vaslav seemed to enjoy talking to them. The very sound of the Russian language seemed to calm him, and he was quieter and happier than he had been for years. One evening, when the troops were singing and dancing, he even got up and danced with them. For their part, they treated him as entirely normal; and this, too, seemed to have its effect on him.

The war ended, and Romola made her way with her cousin Pavel to Vienna where they managed to find a way into the famous Sacher Hotel – windows boarded and doors bolted, for the manager was pretending it was derelict. But the name Nijinsky still meant something to him, and he provided a splendid suite – though he could give them no food. The 75-kilometer journey back to Sopron took them ten days, but finally they managed to get hold of a car, drove back, and fetched Vaslav. Fortunately, there was a sufficient number of balletomanes among the Russian and then the English officers with whom they came into contact to ensure that they were left more or less in peace – and even able to obtain a little food on the black market.

As Vienna began its slow recovery, shops and coffee-houses re-opening, and then the theatres – first the Opera, then the Burgtheater – Nijinsky seemed for a while to recover with it – visiting the art galleries, hearing *Lohengrin* and *The Queen of Spades*, and on one occasion watching the Kirov Ballet – his old company under its new name.

An invitation had been sent to a performance of some kind at the Ronacher Theatre; Romola thought that perhaps it was to be an opera. But then the orchestra began to play the overture to *The Nutcracker*; and onto the stage stepped the great ballerina Galina Ulanova. The performance ended with *Les Sylphides*. As Vaslav watched, he clenched his hands and almost imperceptibly swayed his body with each step. Next day he and Romola called on Ulanova at her hotel; she and her fellow-dancers greeted him tearfully, their arms full of red roses.

During this time, Romola was continually trying to obtain permission to take Nijinsky out of Austria – ideally, to Italy, where Kyra was now living. That proved impossible, but at least they managed to get out of Vienna and into the American zone, where they found refuge in the Gross Glockner Castle, above the Salzach valley. The Chief of the American occupying forces had issued orders that every assistance was to be given them, and the fact that they had access to good supplies of food ensured that they had no difficulty in obtaining servants – including an elderly White Russian officer who became Vaslav's valet. Many new and some former friends came to visit them, and to pay homage to Vaslav, who happily acted the host.

In the winter of 1946/7 Romola went to England, and since her father had been born there (while his family was in exile) was able to obtain a British passport and permission to bring Vaslav to that country. They lived for a while in an hotel at Egham, twenty miles outside London, then in the spring of 1948 moved to a house near Sunningdale, and finally to a house near Arundel.

Karsavina came to visit him, and Madame Legat, the widow of Vaslav's teacher; very occasionally he would speak of his mother (Romola had not told him of her death in 1932, and said she was too old to visit him) or of Bronia; for a time, too, he would look wistfully at a photograph of Kyra, but after a while, when she never appeared, turned it face downward on the drawing-room table.

Occasionally, there would be excursions to London, to the theatre. His critical faculties were still clear, and he made it quite clear when he disapproved of a company; but he did particularly enjoy the dancing of the Indian, Ram Gopal, and that of Luisillo, a Mexican appearing with Carmen Amaya's Flamenco company. Sometimes, the press would hear of his presence, and he would be photographed.

In early 1950 he did not seem well, and his doctor suspected that his kidneys were weak. He was slightly upset when the lease on their house expired, and they were forced to move house – but he liked the small house near Arundel to which they moved, and enjoyed walking in the grounds of the Castle.

In the spring, Serge Lifar, now *maître de ballet* at the Paris Opéra, telephoned to invite Vaslav to be present at a gala performance which he was to organize in order to raise funds for a new grave and monument to the great dancer August Vestris. Nijinsky immediately agreed. When Lifar came to England at the beginning of April with some of his dancers to make a television broadcast from

Alexandra Palace, Vaslav was invited to come to the studios to see them.

Romola met Lifar at the airport, and the following morning – Sunday, 2 April – met Vaslav's train; he waved happily as he saw her on the platform, and that evening they stayed at the Welbeck Hotel, where Lifar came for dinner.

On the morning of Tuesday, 4 April, Vaslav and Romola went to the Wallace Collection, where he stood for some time in front of the Lancret portrait of Camargo. They spent the entire afternoon at the television studios, and he seemed cheerful enough – particularly admiring the dancing of Anna Viroubova. That evening Romola noticed him tapping out dance movements with his fingers as he used to do while choreographing. Then he made the gesture of his left arm over the head which he had made in *Le Spectre de la Rose*.

On the following day he lay on his bed, lethargic but uncomplaining. Next day he was taken to hospital, and went into a coma. On the Saturday he suddenly sat upright and cried 'Mamasha!' In a moment, he was dead.

Karsavina, Sokolova and Marie Rambert were with Romola at the Mass at St James' Russian Church in London; Lifar, Dolin, Cyril Beaumont, Michael Somes, Richard Buckle and the finest of English twentieth century choreographers, Frederick Ashton, were pall-bearers. After a temporary burial at St Marylebone Cemetery the body was carried in 1953 to Paris, where it lies in the Montmartre Cemetery near the body of Vestris.

No film exists of Vaslav Nijinsky dancing. Still photographs, though many of them are fine, give only a faint notion of his genius. His most remarkable ballet, *Le Sacre du Printemps*, is irrecoverable (Stravinsky's score has of course been used by many other choreographers). Marie Rambert believed him to be the first great modern choreographer, and that he was a great dancer is not in question. Yet he danced in public for only ten years.

The legend refuses to die. It gave a charter to the male dancer in the West, who for the first time in over a century became the equal of the ballerina. Many living male dancers have a technique which would enable them to out-dance Nijinsky; it is possible that some might equal him in characterization. But during his brief career he was without peer, dancing, as Cyril Beaumont put it, 'not only with his limbs but with his whole body'.

'I worked like an ox and I lived like a martyr,' Vaslav wrote. One could only compare him with himself. He paid a fearful price for his supremacy. He signed his rambling diary 'God and Nijinsky'. In his time, he was, undeniably, god of the dance.

SELECTED BIBLIOGRAPHY

The most thorough biography of Nijinsky is Richard Buckle's, published in 1971. This was followed by his *Diaghilev* (1979). In these two huge books, Mr Buckle assembles very nearly every known fact, impression, recollection and myth about the Ballets Russes. One or two books have, however, been published since – including, most notably, Nijinsky's sister's biography, *Early Memories* (1981). At times her recollection, in old age, failed her; but an irresistibly vivid picture of her brother emerges from her book.

The following books can be recommended for further reading. The editions given were all published in London, though many are now very difficult to find. *Nijinsky Dancing* (1975), which consists of an album of almost every known photograph of the dancer, with a commentary by Lincoln Kirstein, is particularly recommended.

Beaumont, Cyril: *The Ballet Called Giselle* (1944)
    The Diaghilev Ballet in London (1940)
    Michel Fokine and his Ballets (1935)
    Vaslav Nijinsky (1932)
Benois, Alexandre: *Early Memories of Diaghilev* (in the catalogue of the Diaghilev Exhibition 1954)
    Memoirs, Vol. II (1964)
    Reminiscences of the Russian Ballet (1941)
Bourman, Anatole: *The Tragedy of Nijinsky* (1937)
Buckle, Richard: *In Search of Diaghilev* (1955)
    Nijinsky (1971)
    Diaghilev (1979)
Dandré, Victor: *Anna Pavlova* (1932)

Fokine, Michel: *An Autobiography* (1978)
Grigoriev, S.L.: *The Diaghilev Ballet 1909–29* (1960)
Haskell, Arnold: *Balletomania* (1934)
   Diaghileff (1936)
Johnson, A.E.: *The Russian Ballet* (1913)
Karsavina, Tamara: *Theatre Street* (1930, 1948, 1961)
Kchessinskaya, Mathilda: *Dancing in St Petersburg* (1960)
Kochno, Boris: *Diaghilev and the Ballets Russes* (1971)
Krasovskaya, Vera: *Nijinsky* (1979)
Legat, Nicholas: *Ballets Russes* (1939)
Lifar, Serge: *Serge Diaghilev* (1940)
Macdonald, Nesta: *Diaghilev Observed* (1975)
Magriel, Paul (ed): *Nijinsky* (1948)
Massine, Leonide: *My Life in Ballet* (1968)
Nijinska, Bronislava: *Early Memories* (1981)
Nijinsky, Romola: *Nijinsky* (1933, 1960, 1970)
   The Last Days of Nijinsky (1952)
Nijinsky, Vaslav: *Diary* (1937, 1962)
Propert, W.A.: *The Russian Ballet in Western Europe, 1909–20* (1921)
   The Russian Ballet, 1921–29 (1931)
Reiss, Francoise: *Nijinsky* (1960)
Sokolova, Lydia: *Dancing for Diaghilev* (1960)
Stokes, Adrian: *Tonight the Ballet* (1934)
Stravinsky, Igor: *Chronicle of my Life* (1969)
   Conversations (1959)
   Expositions and Developments (1962)
   Memories and Commentaries (1960)
Whitworth, Geoffrey: *The Art of Nijinsky* (1913)

INDEX

Entries in **bold** denote illustrations, but may also refer to text on the same page.

Alexandrovitch, Grand Duke Vladimir 49
Astruc, Gabriel 49, 55-6, 68-9, 93, 103

Bakst, Leon 40, 41, 42, 47, 50 **59**, 66, 67, 68, 74, **78**, **79**, **81**, 88, 94, 96, 102, 110, 111, **121**, 121, **122**, 141, **175**
Baldina, Alexandre 57
Baton, Rhene- 150
Beaumont, Cyril 13, 66, 80-1, 104, 106-7, 128, 130, 158, 186
Beecham, Sir Thomas 129, **130**
Benois, Alexandre 36, 37, 40, 41, 47, 51, **56-7** 65, 74, 83, 88, 90, 95, 109
Bleuler, Professor 177, 181
'Bluebird' *pas de deux* 37, 48, 59
Bolm, Adolph 59, 86, 90, 93, 103, 129, 138, 153, 161
Bourman, Anatole 34, 40
Buckle, Richard 13, 79, 143, 159, 178, 186
Butt, Alfred 156, 158

Calmette, Gaston 125-6
Carnaval 75, 76, 85, 87, 96, **102**, **103**, 112, 115, 138, 163
Cecchetti, Enrico 18, 24, 39, 60, 81, 95, 103, 138, 139, 149, 159
Chaliapin, Feodor 26, 42, 55, 67, 69
Checkmate 10

Chopiniana 44; see also *Les Sylphides*
Cléopâtre 47, 76, **53**, 66, 76
Cocteau, Jean 55, 69, 80, 104, 105, 110, **123**, 144, **147**, 159
Cunard, Lady 79

Danse Siamoise 85
Debussy, Claude 9, 119, 141, 143
Diaghilev, Sergei Pavlovitch 9, 10, 40-154, **41**, 158, 159, 162, 164, 165, 170, 171, 172, **173**, 178, 180
Dolin, Anton 44-5, 179, 180, 186
Don Giovanni 32
Duncan, Isadora 31, 35, 55, 68, 74, 141, 164-5

Ephrussy, Maurice 67

Fedorova, Anna 31
Feodorova, Sophie 59
Fedorovna, Dowager Empress Maria 91
Filosofov, Dmitri 41, 44
Fokine, Michel 14, 24, 28 30, 36, 37, 47, 48, 50, 53, 73, 75, 76, 95, 96, 98, 99, 101-2, 105, 116, 120-1, 126, 127, 129, 147, 152, 155, 159
Frazer, Grace Lovat 13, 106
Fredericks, Count 91

Gerdt, Pavel 27, 47
Gerdt, Yelizaveta 33

Giselle **70**, **73**, 74, 82-3, **84**, 88ff, 96, 115
Grigoriev, Sergei Leonidovitch 75, 95, 120, 154, 173
Gunsburg, Baron Dmitri 150, 151

Hahn, Reynaldo 69, 79, 82, 110, 121

Idzikowsky, Stanislas 13, 99
Imperial Theatre School 24ff

Jeux 10, 14, 133, 134, 141, **142**, 145, **146**
Johnson and Johnson 22, 38
Jones, Robert Edmund 165, 167

Karalli, Vera 54, 56
Karsavina, Tamara 13, 17, 24, 36, 44, 48, 52, 55, 57, 58, 59, 60-1, **67**, 74, 75, 76, 77, 82-3, 89, 90, 93, **95**, **97**, **98**, 99, 103, 113, 122, 129, 134, **137**, 141, **142**, **144**, 185, 186
Kchessinskaya, Mathilda 24, 33, 36, 37, 39, 49, 71, 89, 92, 115, 156
Khan, Otto 165
Kochno, Boris 63, 83
Kostrovsky, Dmitri 169, 171, 172, 173
Krasnoe Selo, 34
Krasovskaya, Vera 13, 38, 82

Krupensky, Alexander 32, 91
Kyasht, Lydia 36, 37, 52, 112

La Fille Mal Gardée 36
L'Après-midi d'un Faune 9, 65, 89, 101, 117ff, **118**, 122ff, **123, 124, 125, 127, 128, 129**, 136, 157, 161, 167, 171
Le Dieu Bleu 69, 94, 103, 116, 121-2, 136, **137**
Le Festin **4**, 48, **59** 59-60, **60**
Legat, Nicholas 27, 30, 35, 71
Legat, Sergei 25, 27, 30
Le Pavillon d'Armide **12**, 36, 38, 44, 47, 49, 51, **56-7, 58**, 103, 112-13
Le Sacre du Printemps 10, 88, 135ff, **139, 142**, 143ff
Les Orientales 74, 85,
Le Spectre de la Rose 9, 94, 96-100, **97, 98, 99, 100**, 105, 108, 112, 121, 144, 158, 163, 171, 174
Les Sylphides 9, 47, 50, **51**, 63-4, 65, 72, 130, 157
Le Talisman 71-2, **72**
Liadov, Anatole 73
Lifar, Serge 179, 185, 186
Little Tich 67, 131
Lopokova, Lydia 93
Lvov, Prince Pavel Dmitrievitch 13, 38ff, 51-2, 67, 130

Markus, Emilia 138, 154, 160-1, 162, 177
Massine, Leonide 60, 156, 159, 161-2, 163, 171
Mavrine, Alexis 52, 64
Monteux, Pierre 105, 144, 165, 167
Mordkin, Mikhail 9
Morrell, Lady Ottoline 131, 132, 133, 157

Narcisse 94, 101-2, 105, 163
Nelidova, Lydia 120
Nijinska, Bronislava Fominitchna ('Bronia', sister) 10, **28** 32, 35, 38, 39, 48, 52, 75, 90-1, 93, 130, 134, 151, 154, 156, 178
Nijinska, Eleanora Nicolaevna ('Liota') (mother) **19**, 21ff, 52, 91, 130, 134, 154, 178, 185
Nijinska, Kyra (daughter) 159, 160, 162, 174, 175-6, **178**, 180, 185
Nijinska, Romola (wife) 10, 138, 145, **148**, 149ff, **153**, 162
Nijinska, Stanislas Fomitch ('Stassik', brother) 21, 28, 35, 134, 175
Nijinska, Tamara (daughter) 178
Nijinsky, Thomas Lavrentievitch ('Foma', father) 19, **20**, 21ff, 32, 34, 134, 135
Nijinsky, Vaslav Fomitch ('Vatsa')
  in America 164
  as artist **114**, 175, 180
  and the arts 65, 68
  balletic technique 50, 53-4, 58, 60, 63-4, 66, 81-3, 87, 104, 106-7, 130, 173-4
  ballet notation 170
  characterization 57, **62**, 72, 80, 82, 99-100, 104, 106-8, 110, 128, 163-4
  as choreographer 10, 17, 33, 75, 88, 101, 111, 117, 119, 122ff, 135 139-40, 145, 146-7, 167
  as dandy 38-9
  diary of 44, 108, 180
  dismissal by Diaghilev 154-5

and dreadful costumes 65, **73**, 98, 99, 142
engagement 151
expelled from school 29
final public performance 176-7
finances 155, 156, 159 162, 172
in *Firebird* 84
first Paris season 51ff
first public appearance 21
flamenco 170
graduation 33-4
and human rights 30
and humour 132-3, 167
illness 158
'indecent' costume 91-2
intelligence 109-10, 111, 132
last stage performance 174
and leaps 17, 31, 37, 51, 58, 60-1, 63, 72, 80, 97-9, 110, 112, 174, 181
leaves Russia 94-5
madness 168ff
make-up 99, 102, 106-7
marriage 153
meets Diaghilev 40, 43-4
military service 89, 116, 156, 168
mime 82
musicality 28, 120, 121, 140, **146**
physical appearance 109-10, 112, 138, 179-10
physical energy 28-9, 151
personality 131, 132, 165
at school 23ff
school performances 27, 31, 33
serious accident 26
sexuality 13, 14, 35, 39, 40, 44-5, 61-2, 108-9, 126, 133, 150, 154
strength 54, 60
sunstroke 88-9
typhoid 67
venereal disease 39, 45
views on the ballet 47, 111, 140
Noailles, Countess Anna de 63

191

Nureyev, Rudolf 61, 82, 97

Oboukhov, Mikhail 17, 27, 30, 31

Paquita **52**
Pardany, Oscar (father-in-law) 177
Pavlova, Anna 18, 24, 32, 37, **43**, 44, 47, 48, 50, **55**, 72, 84, 88, 112, 115, 116, 157, 167
Pedorova, Olga 64
Petipa, Marius 18, 24, 36
Petrushka 9, 22-3, 88, 94, 103, 105-8, **106, 107, 108, 109**, 136, 163, 179
Pilz, Maria 108
Poiret, Paul 79
Polovtsian Dances 48, 58-9, 86
Preobrajenskaya, Olga 41, 44, 47
Pulszky, Madame *see* Markus, Emilia
Pulszky, Romola de *see* Nijinska, Romola

Rachmaninov, Serge 38, 42
Rambert, Dame Marie 9, 13, 17, 61, 104, 126, 128, 136, **139** 143, 154, 178, 186
Ravel, Maurice 146
Raymonda 32
Redon, Odilon 125
Ricketts, Charles 102
Rimsky-Korsakov, Nicholas 38, 42, 74, 77
Ripon, Lady 13, 131, 159, 160, 161
Rite of Spring see *Le Sacre du Printemps*
Rodin, Auguste 125, 134
Roerich, Nicholas 47, 59, 135, **142**
'Roses and Butterflies' see *Don Giovanni*
Rubenstein, Ida 48, **53** 64, 66, 76, 80, 81, 117
Rumiantseva, 23, 35

Sargent, John Singer **12** 114
Schéhérazade 68, 74, 76ff, **78, 79, 81** 94, **95**, 96, 103, 115, 153, 162, 163, 171
Schollar, Ludmilla 141, **143, 144**
Sedova, Julia 34, 36
Serov, Valentin **68**
Sert, Misia, and banana 63
Setov, Josef Yakovelevitch 21, 22
Sitwell, Sir Osbert 107-8, 132
Sitwell, Sir Sacheverell 13
Sokolova, Lydia 111, 128, 132, 143, 166-7, 168-9, 180
Strachey, Lytton 131, 146
Strauss, Richard 152, 159, 160, 161
Stravinsky, Igor 28, 65, **69** 72ff, 88, 103, 120-1, 140, **147**
Svetlov, Valentin **55**

Tcherepnine, Nicholas 36, 47, 57, 73
Teliakovsky, Colonel V. A. 71, 84, 89, 92
Till Eulenspiegel 160, 161, 165ff, **167, 168**

Vassili, 50, 105, 116, 154
Vestris, Auguste 9, 55, 63, 185
Volonsky, Prince Sergei 41

Zverev, Nicolas 169, 171